Meditate So You Can Elevate

How To Keep Going Up When
Life Is Pulling You Down

Rev. Dr. James E. Jones, Jr.

authorHOUSE®

AuthorHouse™
1663 Liberty Drive
Bloomington, IN 47403
www.authorhouse.com
Phone: 1-800-839-8640

First published by AuthorHouse 3/31/2011

ISBN: 978-1-4567-4713-8 (hc)
ISBN: 978-1-4567-5278-1 (e)
ISBN: 978-1-4567-4714-5 (sc)

Library of Congress Control Number: 2011903739

Printed in the United States of America

Any people depicted in stock imagery provided by Thinkstock are models,
and such images are being used for illustrative purposes only.
Certain stock imagery © Thinkstock.

This book is printed on acid-free paper.

Table of Contents

Dedication

This book is dedicated to God, who gave me the vision. I am grateful to my spiritual mentor, Dr. Joe Ratliff, whose leadership, friendship and patience has elevated me to this level. Thank you for never being too big or too busy to take a moment to impart some spiritual truths in my life. I recognize you did not have to, so I am forever grateful that you did.

To my partner in marriage and ministry, Cheryl, thank you for your love and support through the good, bad, pretty and ugly. To my daughter Jarae', "Wow! You are simply amazing. Guess what..."

To my mother, Mary Jones Turner, my drive to never give up I got from you. To my sister Janelle, thank you for forcing me to be better and stronger each day.

Finally, this book is dedicated to the late James E. Jones, Sr. On October 16, 1990, a huge hole was left in my heart when you died. Thank you because your death broke me but it also blessed me. I would not be where I am today without you. Thank you for an awesome but brief journey together. Your death forever keeps me humbled.

Acknowledgements

Over the years, I have met the most incredible people. I would like to sincerely thank many of the individuals who have suffered and celebrated with me.

I am grateful for my time at the Abyssinia Baptist Church in Norfolk, Virginia and Dr. Frank Guns, Pastor Emeritus, Dr. Sheridan Nelson, Union Bethel Baptist Church of Chesapeake, Virginia, Dr. John Guns, Gethsemone Community Fellowship Baptist Church in Norfolk, Virginia, Dr. Kirk Houston, Fifth Street Baptist Church, Dr. F. Todd Gray of Richmond, Virginia, Mount Olive Baptist Church in Lewiston, North Carolina, First Baptist Church West Munden of Chesapeake, Virginia, Mount Lebanon Baptist Church in Chesapeake, Virginia and Bishop Kim Brown. To the Grace Fellowship Worship Center Family and our leaders: Shaq, Karen Bell, Kecia, James Burton, Macy Church, Rose Summerville, Kavoris Fruster and Slater Johnson. I love you all 4 life. Thank you all for loving me the way you do.

I am also grateful to my many professors at Virginia Union School of Theology, Norfolk State University, and Southern Baptist Theological Seminary. To my strong supporting cast of friends: Dr. Steve Blunt, Rev. Kevin Williams, Dr. Peter Wherry, Rev. Anthony Ferebee, Dr. Jerome Williams, Dr. Vernard Hinton, Lisa Buffaloe, Nicole Ballance, Tanya and Derrick Hagan, Pat and Fran, Jamila Kimbrough, Jay Jones, Ron Bellard (Big Mac), Rhynda Riddick (AKA Deacon Jesse), Oliver and Tasha Holley, Chaplain Doug Watson and Linda Hudson, both of Riverside Medical Center. To my coaches of encouragement, Shaq Heckstall, Tony Church and James Church, thank you guys for making me stronger and better.

To my Executive Assistant, Abbey Askew, your commitment to

excellence continues to push me to strive to be better today than I was yesterday. I am also grateful for your editing assistance. One day I will graduate from the legal pad to the computer, but not just yet (smile).

I am also grateful to all of the people who help make this dream a reality by either blessing me or breaking me. I couldn't have made it without you. I'm stronger and wiser.

To my JEJ marketing team: Tony Stokes, Ebonie Davis, Terrell Heckstall, Veronica Robinson and Tyree Miller, thanks for using your gifts.

Finally, this book was written for individuals who have been battered, bruised or broken by the pressures of life or the other people in your life. May this book become the bridge to move you from being broken to living blessed. No matter how bad it hurts, you are a survivor.

If I did not list your name, this thank you is to Lottie, Dottie and everybody!

Foreword

A senior pastor is discussing serious matters with the senior members of his church when one his members comments about her sleepless night. She remarks how she is tired of counting sheep. Immediately, another senior chides her for counting sheep when she could "talk to the Shepherd.

While serving as a visiting professor at Southern Baptist Theological Seminary in Louisville, Kentucky, I had the privilege of meeting James Jones the doctoral student. He exhibited an inquisitive mind, a sensitive heart and a caring spirit! I followed his career and witnessed his maturity in faith and practice.

From the very first entry, "Love doesn't hurt," you quickly detect a sensitivity that reveals a cognitive transparency.

How refreshing to discover a writer whose head and heart blend so well to the point that each of the entries become conversational.

As a pastor I am often told by members that I must have bugged their homes because the sermon was directed toward them. Several of these daily words become disturbingly close to our private thoughts and experiences. These entries help us to get beyond "What's up!" We know what's up and quickly know what's going down.

The use of scriptures simply wet our appetites for more! This encourages the reader to explore the verses before and after the selected text. Aristotle was the devoted student of Plato. He once said "Plato is dear to me, but dearer still is truth." We must prize truth above all other things. No person must be dearer to us than the truth. No goal must be greater than to know the truth and no objective greater than to tell the truth. Everyone who reads this book will find hope for the journey.

Every page of this book reflects truth! Join Dr. Jones on this journey of revealed truth. Be careful because the truth will set you free!

Dr. Joe Samuel Ratliff, Pastor
Brentwood Baptist Church
Houston, TX

Daily Devotionals

Love Doesn't Hurt

Romans 13:10 (New International Version)
¹⁰Love does no harm to its neighbor. Therefore love is the fulfillment of the law.

Recently, I was engaged in a conversation with a young lady who suggested that one of her friends was involved in a sexually abusive relationship. She continued to tell me that the man in the relationship used the Bible to justify and support his case. He would consistently argue that this woman was his personal slave and as such, was supposed to do whatever he wanted even if it was against her own will.

I would offer today that you be careful about getting submission and abuse confused. So often in life, people mistreat us, take advantage of us, and abuse us all in the name of love. I believe Tina Turner was right when she raised the question, "What's love got to do with it?" Love may not be perfect but it is not wrapped in pain either. How long are you going to watch someone you love destroy you, all in the name of love? Could it be the person who is trapped in the dark side of love is you?

Let's be great today.

Rev. Dr. James E. Jones, Jr.

Take Somebody With You

2 Corinthians 13:1-4 (New International Version)
Final Warnings

¹This will be my third visit to you. "Every matter must be established by the testimony of two or three witnesses." ²I already gave you a warning when I was with you the second time. I now repeat it while absent: On my return I will not spare those who sinned earlier or any of the others, ³since you are demanding proof that Christ is speaking through me. He is not weak in dealing with you, but is powerful among you. ⁴For to be sure, he was crucified in weakness, yet he lives by God's power. Likewise, we are weak in him, yet by God's power we will live with him to serve you.

Trouble is easy to get into but hard to get out of. That phrase brings to mind an important meeting I once had with a certain individual regarding the allegation that he was spreading rumors throughout the community, as well as in the church. During the meeting, this individual said something that will stick with me for the rest of my life. His exact words were, "When it's just me and you, it's your word against mine." Although he openly admitted that he had started the rumors during our private meeting, he would never admit it publicly.

Life is filled with these kinds of individuals. You know them…the ones who throw rocks and hide their hands. Be careful how you settle disputes. Try not to settle them alone. When you travel with a witness, it becomes your word against theirs.

Today, let's be victorious together.

Coping with Stress

Philippians 4:6-13 (New International Version)

6Do not be anxious about anything, but in everything, by prayer and petition, with thanksgiving, present your requests to God. 7And the peace of God, which transcends all understanding, will guard your hearts and your minds in Christ Jesus.

8Finally, brothers, whatever is true, whatever is noble, whatever is right, whatever is pure, whatever is lovely, whatever is admirable—if anything is excellent or praiseworthy—think about such things. 9Whatever you have learned or received or heard from me, or seen in me—put it into practice. And the God of peace will be with you.

Thanks for Their Gifts

10I rejoice greatly in the Lord that at last you have renewed your concern for me. Indeed, you have been concerned, but you had no opportunity to show it. 11I am not saying this because I am in need, for I have learned to be content whatever the circumstances. 12I know what it is to be in need, and I know what it is to have plenty. I have learned the secret of being content in any and every situation, whether well fed or hungry, whether living in plenty or in want. 13I can do everything through him who gives me strength.

I'm sure you've heard many people say, "I am too blessed to be stressed!" Although that may be true with some of us, it is not the case with everyone. My question to you today is what do you do when your blessing is the cause of the stress? Here are a few things you can implement the next time you are feeling stressed out.

1. Step away and do something fun for yourself.
2. Don't take yourself or others too seriously.
3. Remember, you have a right to be concerned but not consumed.
4. Don't kill yourself trying to do it all by yourself.
5. Find a quiet place throughout the day and read His word.
6. Don't let anybody live in your head for free.
7. Eat healthy.

8. Exercise regularly. Force yourself to if you have to. You will feel better.
9. Ask yourself if it will matter 30 days from now.
10. Most importantly, PRAY, PRAY and PRAY. If you are still stressed, then PRAY, PRAY and PRAY some more!

Remember, this too shall pass

You Can Do It

Joshua 1:7-9 (New International Version)
⁷ Be strong and very courageous. Be careful to obey all the law my servant Moses gave you; do not turn from it to the right or to the left, that you may be successful wherever you go. ⁸ Do not let this Book of the Law depart from your mouth; meditate on it day and night, so that you may be careful to do everything written in it. Then you will be prosperous and successful. ⁹ Have I not commanded you? Be strong and courageous. Do not be terrified; do not be discouraged, for the LORD your God will be with you wherever you go."

Life is filled with ups and downs. There are haters and critics everywhere. There will always be at least one person, who is either hating on you or jealous of you, who feels it is their divine responsibility to tell you what you can't do or what you can't become. The next time one of these individuals seek to move around in your space or get close to you, don't subscribe to their negative press. Instead, become like Joshua. Believe that you can go where nobody else has gone, do what nobody else has done and possess what nobody else has possessed. You may be asking yourself, "If nobody else has done it before, why should I think I am going to do it?" God is always waiting for the right person at the right time. This time, it's you. You can do it. You are a champion.

Rev. Dr. James E. Jones, Jr.

Keep Your Eyes Open

Matthew 25:31-40 (New International Version)
The Sheep and the Goats

³¹"When the Son of Man comes in his glory, and all the angels with him, he will sit on his throne in heavenly glory. ³²All the nations will be gathered before him, and he will separate the people one from another as a shepherd separates the sheep from the goats. ³³He will put the sheep on his right and the goats on his left. ³⁴"Then the King will say to those on his right, 'Come, you who are blessed by my Father; take your inheritance, the kingdom prepared for you since the creation of the world. ³⁵For I was hungry and you gave me something to eat, I was thirsty and you gave me something to drink, I was a stranger and you invited me in, ³⁶I needed clothes and you clothed me, I was sick and you looked after me, I was in prison and you came to visit me.' ³⁷"Then the righteous will answer him, 'Lord, when did we see you hungry and feed you, or thirsty and give you something to drink? ³⁸When did we see you a stranger and invite you in, or needing clothes and clothe you? ³⁹When did we see you sick or in prison and go to visit you?' ⁴⁰"The King will reply, 'I tell you the truth, whatever you did for one of the least of these brothers of mine, you did for me.'

Oftentimes we miss precious opportunities to be a blessing to others simply because we overlook them. The person who needs a hug doesn't always look broken. The person who doesn't have enough money to get something to eat does not always look desperate. Sometimes those who need it the most are standing around us, sitting near us or live close by. Don't miss an opportunity today to be a blessing in somebody's life because you overlooked them. Keep your eyes open today so that not only will you be impressed with their outer appearance but your view of them will reach their soul. Today, may God grant you the vision to see exactly what is going on with others. Today, may He allow you to not only see others but to look through others. You must keep your eyes open or you may just miss your blessing. Stay focused on the Saviour and not your surroundings.

He's Still the Same

Hebrews 13:8 (New International Version)
⁸Jesus Christ is the same yesterday and today and forever.

Everything around us seems to change. Relationships change, our addresses change, our phone numbers change, our jobs change but God never changes. So many times we talk about God as if He is some abstract being who is intentionally avoiding us. Truthfully, God is waiting on you in the same place you left Him. If you're having problems locating Him, it's not because He has moved...maybe you have. God hasn't gotten a U-Haul - maybe you have?

ᡧᡧᡧᡧᡧᡧᡧᡧᡧᡧᡧᡧᡧᡧᡧᡧᡧ

You Are Going to Need More Room

Psalm 18:19 (New International Version)
¹⁹ He brought me out into a spacious place, he rescued me because he delighted in me.

I can't speak for you, but one of my least favorite past times is moving. The process of moving seems like an endless discovery of things you had forgotten about. Sometimes our lives are like that process. God can remove something and for some reason we replace it. This is going to be your season of expansion. God is going to bless you like never before. Even as you are reading this, start clearing out space because the place you have reserved for your blessing is simply not big enough. You're going to need more room. Increase is in your mouth.

Rev. Dr. James E. Jones, Jr.

Be Like Jesus

Ephesians 5:11-14 (New International Version)
[11]Have nothing to do with the fruitless deeds of darkness, but rather expose them. [12]For it is shameful even to mention what the disobedient do in secret. [13]But everything exposed by the light becomes visible, [14]for it is light that makes everything visible. This is why it is said: "Wake up, O sleeper, rise from the dead, and Christ will shine on you."

Several years ago, one of the biggest ad campaigns was the Nike campaign "Be Like Mike" referring to the legendary Michael Jordan. As great as Michael Jordan is, not even his greatness could prevent him from having to face some of life's greatest challenges.

So if you are looking for someone to pattern yourself after, I recommend Jesus. He is the only person I know who was always surrounded by sin but remained sinless. Try to be like Jesus today.

Save Me From Me

Romans 7:21-25 (New International Version)
[21]So I find this law at work: When I want to do good, evil is right there with me. [22]For in my inner being I delight in God's law; [23]but I see another law at work in the members of my body, waging war against the law of my mind and making me a prisoner of the law of sin at work within my members. [24]What a wretched man I am! Who will rescue me from this body of death? [25]Thanks be to God—through Jesus Christ our Lord! So then, I myself in my mind am a slave to God's law, but in the sinful nature a slave to the law of sin.

I am convinced that for many of us we are our own worst enemy. For some of us, there is a constant battle between good and evil and right and wrong. God has blessed you with so much that sometimes it is hard for you to believe

In spite of all of the blessings, we still find ourselves struggling with the issues of life. You know your tomorrow looks much better than your yesterday. The only person who can mess that up is you. Today my prayer for you is that God will save you from you.

Don't be your own worst enemy today.

সৈ সৈ সৈ সৈ সৈ সৈ সৈ সৈ সৈ সৈ সৈ সৈ সৈ সৈ সৈ সৈ

What Kind of Fruit Are You Bearing?

Galatians 5:22-23 (New International Version)
²²But the fruit of the Spirit is love, joy, peace, patience, kindness, goodness, faithfulness, ²³gentleness and self-control. Against such things there is no law.

It has been stated that you will know a tree by the fruit it bears. If that is true, then a lot of people in the world are producing rotten fruit. Some of us could use attitude adjustments, our conversation could be more positive and pleasant and even the way we look sometimes sends a negative message. Try today to exemplify fresh fruit, beautiful fruit or healthy fruit. Have a winning attitude. If somebody were to shake your tree right now, what kind of fruit would fall off?

Let's be great.

What Is Your Issue?

John 4:28-32 (New International Version)
²⁸Then, leaving her water jar, the woman went back to the town and said to the people, ²⁹"Come, see a man who told me everything I ever did. Could this be the Christ?" ³⁰They came out of the town and made their way toward him. ³¹Meanwhile his disciples urged him, "Rabbi, eat something." ³²But he said to them, "I have food to eat that you know nothing about."

All of us have to struggle or fight against something. Whether it's lust, loneliness, low self-esteem, depression or anger, we all have our own personal challenges. The problem with having an issue is not acknowledgement but avoidance. Too many of us run from who we authentically are in hopes that we can "outrun" it before it catches up to us. We end up spending a lot of energy and time running from the very thing or person that is our issue. God knows our issues and loves us with them.

This is the season God is calling us to be authentically who He has created us to be. It is time for us to remove the mask and all levels of falsehood. Be who God knows who you are today.

Handling Hardships

2 Timothy 2:1-3 (New International Version)
¹You then, my son, be strong in the grace that is in Christ Jesus. ²And the things you have heard me say in the presence of many witnesses entrust to reliable men who will also be qualified to teach others. ³Endure hardship with us like a good soldier of Christ Jesus.

Over the last decade our world has seen its share of disasters and hardships. From floods to earthquakes, we have experienced tremendous misfortunes. For some of us, hardships are not about earthquakes, hurricanes or global misfortunes. It is more about just trying to survive everyday hardships like handling adversity at the workplace, dealing with a relationship gone bad, raising children without a support system or having more BILLS than money. As you ask yourself how to handle these hardships, remember two important things:

1. Simply endure it. Some stuff you just have to learn how to keep pushing through even when you get tired.
2. Go through it knowing that you are going to come out of it. Know that if you can't handle it, He can.

Remember, the greater the test the greater the reward.

Rev. Dr. James E. Jones, Jr.

In God We Trust

Psalm 56 (New International Version)

¹ Be merciful to me, O God, for men hotly pursue me; all day long they press their attack. ² My slanderers pursue me all day long; many are attacking me in their pride. ³ When I am afraid, I will trust in you. ⁴ In God, whose word I praise, in God I trust; I will not be afraid. What can mortal man do to me? ⁵ All day long they twist my words; they are always plotting to harm me. ⁶ They conspire, they lurk, they watch my steps, eager to take my life. ⁷ On no account let them escape; in your anger, O God, bring down the nations. ⁸ Record my lament; list my tears on your scroll are they not in your record? ⁹ Then my enemies will turn back when I call for help. By this I will know that God is for me. ¹⁰ In God, whose word I praise, in the LORD, whose word I praise- ¹¹ in God I trust; I will not be afraid. What can man do to me? ¹² I am under vows to you, O God; I will present my thank offerings to you. ¹³ For you have delivered me from death and my feet from stumbling, that I may walk before God in the light of life.

Do you ever feel like it is just you against the world? Does it seem like everywhere you turn there is someone plotting your downfall? When your enemies are all around you watching and hanging on your every word, trust God to not only protect you from them, but to prosper you in spite of them. In God we trust needs to mean more to you than a phrase on the back of your money. It needs to become your verbal declaration. Trust God today. He can handle everything and everyone else.

Trust God no matter what.

The Power of Prayer

James 5:16 (New International Version)
¹⁶Therefore confess your sins to each other and pray for each other so that you may be healed. The prayer of a righteous man is powerful and effective.

The other day, I saw a big truck at a gas station. Evidently the battery had died and the truck needed a jump. After briefly watching the driver's tireless efforts of trying to start the truck, a group of us pushed it off to the side of the road. A few seconds later, a small sports car zoomed up and asked if we needed a jump. In my mind, I was wondering how such a small car was going to be able to get this huge truck started.

We placed the cables from the sports car onto the truck's battery and with one turn of the key, the truck started flawlessly. Sensing my confusion, the owner of the sports car said, "It may be small but there is a lot of power underneath the hood." That is what prayer is, power underneath your hood. Prayer still changes things.

Rev. Dr. James E. Jones, Jr.

A God Who Answers

Psalm 101:1-2 (New International Version)
*¹ I will sing of your love and justice; to you, O LORD, I will sing praise. ²
I will be careful to lead a blameless life— when will you come to me? I will
walk in my house with blameless heart*

I know several people who don't answer phone calls from numbers they
don't recognize. Then I know some people who will only talk to you
when it fits into their schedule. I also know people who don't answer
their phones no matter what time of day you call. I am so thankful that
God is not like any of these individuals. God is an always available God.
No matter what you've done or where you've been, God is only a call in
your heart away. He is the God who hears you when you call.

God is always on the other line waiting for you to pick up.

Less Becomes Greater

John 3:25-30 (New International Version)
²⁵An argument developed between some of John's disciples and a certain Jew over the matter of ceremonial washing. ²⁶They came to John and said to him, "Rabbi, that man who was with you on the other side of the Jordan—the one you testified about—well, he is baptizing, and everyone is going to him." ²⁷To this John replied, "A man can receive only what is given him from heaven. ²⁸You yourselves can testify that I said, 'I am not the Christ but am sent ahead of him.' ²⁹The bride belongs to the bridegroom. The friend who attends the bridegroom waits and listens for him, and is full of joy when he hears the bridegroom's voice. That joy is mine, and it is now complete. ³⁰He must become greater; I must become less.

In our world, we tend to think that greater is better or that bigger is better. That leads to a never ending quest for bigger things, more money and titles of authority. Let me flip the script and suggest that bigger does not always mean better. As we look closely at Jesus, He did not come to be served but to serve. As he willingly served, God willingly promoted Him to a place on the right side. Good things happen to those who learn how to serve others.

Things don't make you. You make the things. Live like it.

Rev. Dr. James E. Jones, Jr.

I'm Not Going to Lose My Mind

Isaiah 26:3-4 (New International Version)
³You will keep in perfect peace him whose mind is steadfast, because he trusts in you. ⁴Trust in the LORD forever, for the LORD, the LORD, is the Rock eternal.

Sometimes life can get so crazy you literally feel like you are about to lose your mind. Don't let the cares of the world, the pressure of who you are and the inconsistencies of others drive you crazy. In the middle of chaos, there is perfect peace in Jesus. When you feel as if your mind is on its way out, remember:

1. Realize you must trust Him even when you can't trace Him.
2. Recognize God will straighten all the crooked places in your life.
3. Remember today is a good day to shout it out. Go ahead and shout!

Free your spirit and your mind will follow.

When What You Do is Not Enough

1 Corinthians 13:1-8 (New International Version)
Love

¹If I speak in the tongues of men and of angels, but have not love, I am only a resounding gong or a clanging cymbal. ²If I have the gift of prophecy and can fathom all mysteries and all knowledge, and if I have a faith that can move mountains, but have not love, I am nothing. ³If I give all I possess to the poor and surrender my body to the flames, but have not love, I gain nothing. ⁴Love is patient, love is kind. It does not envy, it does not boast, it is not proud. ⁵It is not rude, it is not self-seeking, it is not easily angered, it keeps no record of wrongs. ⁶Love does not delight in evil but rejoices with the truth. ⁷It always protects, always trusts, always hopes, always perseveres. ⁸Love never fails. But where there are prophecies, they will cease; where there are tongues, they will be stilled; where there is knowledge, it will pass away.

There are times when you just can't do enough to satisfy a person. No matter how hard you try, what you do just never seems to be enough. Before you get frustrated and depressed wondering what you could have done differently, consider that maybe the problem is not you but them. Don't blame yourself. Just recognize they need to learn how to love themselves before they can love you. Before you can love right, you have to love yourself first.

Rev. Dr. James E. Jones, Jr.

Good Things Come to Those Who Wait

Isaiah 40:28-31 (New International Version)

²⁸ Do you not know? Have you not heard? The LORD is the everlasting God, the Creator of the ends of the earth. He will not grow tired or weary, and his understanding no one can fathom. ²⁹ He gives strength to the weary and increases the power of the weak. ³⁰ Even youths grow tired and weary, and young men stumble and fall, ³¹ but those who hope in the LORD will renew their strength. They will soar on wings like eagles; they will run and not grow weary, they will walk and not be faint.

We live in a microwave generation that is dominated by fast food and fast living. However, there are some blessings and miracles that are worth waiting for. God is not preparing your next blessing out of a box that can be placed in a microwave. Your next blessing is being made from scratch. It has all of your favorite ingredients in it and even some stuff you don't like. When it's all said and done, you'll love it. So while you wait remember:

1. It's your season of renewal.
2. It's your season of release.
3. It's your season of recovery.

Go out today and have the best day of your life.

Stop Running

Jonah 1:3 (New International Version)
³ But Jonah ran away from the LORD and headed for Tarshish. He went down to Joppa, where he found a ship bound for that port. After paying the fare, he went aboard and sailed for Tarshish to flee from the LORD.

Growing up, I used to play games like Freeze Tag and Hide and Go Seek. These games were fun and all about not getting caught. I have discovered that Hide and Go Seek is still a very popular game. The only problem is that people are running and hiding from God. God has created you with a purpose and God is expecting you to fulfill the assignment He has for your life. Nobody but you can do what he created you to do. I know that sometimes you may not want to do what God is calling you to do. There may be times where you wonder if God even has the right person for the job. Let me assure you that God is looking for you. You are too slow to out run God so stop running!

When God Is Silent

Habakkuk 1:13 (New International Version)

13Your eyes are too pure to look on evil; you cannot tolerate wrong. Why then do you tolerate the treacherous? Why are you silent while the wicked swallow up those more righteous than themselves?

Today you may be feeling as though the communication between you and God has been temporarily disconnected. You call Him but all you get in return is complete silence. What do you do when God is silent?

First, get an overhead view of your situation. You can see more in an airplane than you can in a car. Secondly, know that God reserves the right to answer whenever He gets ready. Most importantly, remember to walk by faith and not by sight.

Silence does not mean absence.

God Never Fails

Lamentations 3:20-26 (New International Version)
[20]I well remember them, and my soul is downcast within me. [21]Yet this I call to mind and therefore I have hope: [22]Because of the LORD's great love we are not consumed, for his compassions never fail. [23]They are new every morning, great is your faithfulness. [24]I say to myself, "The LORD is my portion, therefore I will wait for him." [25]The LORD is good to those whose hope is in him, to the one who seeks him, [26]it is good to wait quietly for the salvation of the LORD.

Not much in life is guaranteed anymore. People fail us, computers crash, cars break down and eventually no matter how good what you have is, sooner or later it will have to be replaced. When you hook up with God, you get a lifetime guarantee that nothing will be able to separate you from His love. Don't give up on God because God will stand with you and He will not fail. When others have let you down, God will be right there to reassure you. In every situation you will prevail because God never fails.

God has guaranteed you victory today.

Rev. Dr. James E. Jones, Jr.

Wait On God

Isaiah 30 (New International Version)
Woe to the Obstinate Nation

[1]"Woe to the obstinate children," declares the LORD, "to those who carry out plans that are not mine, forming an alliance, but not by my Spirit, heaping sin upon sin, [2]who go down to Egypt without consulting me; who look for help to Pharaoh's protection, to Egypt's shade for refuge. [3]But Pharaoh's protection will be to your shame, Egypt's shade will bring you disgrace. [4]Though they have officials in Zoan and their envoys have arrived in Hanes, [5]everyone will be put to shame because of a people useless to them, who bring neither help nor advantage, but only shame and disgrace." [6]An oracle concerning the animals of the Negev: Through a land of hardship and distress, of lions and lionesses, of adders and darting snakes, the envoys carry their riches on donkeys' backs, their treasures on the humps of camels, to that unprofitable nation, [7]to Egypt, whose help is utterly useless. Therefore I call her Rahab the Do-Nothing. [8]Go now, write it on a tablet for them, inscribe it on a scroll, that for the days to come it may be an everlasting witness. [9]These are rebellious people, deceitful children, children unwilling to listen to the LORD's instruction. [10]They say to the seers, "See no more visions!" and to the prophets, "Give us no more visions of what is right! Tell us pleasant things, prophesy illusions. [11]Leave this way, get off this path, and stop confronting us with the Holy One of Israel!" [12]Therefore, this is what the Holy One of Israel says: "Because you have rejected this message, relied on oppression and depended on deceit, [13]this sin will become for you like a high wall, cracked and bulging, that collapses suddenly, in an instant. [14]It will break in pieces like pottery, shattered so mercilessly that among its pieces not a fragment will be found for taking coals from a hearth or scooping water out of a cistern." [15]This is what the Sovereign LORD, the Holy One of Israel, says: "In repentance and rest is your salvation, in quietness and trust is your strength, but you would have none of it. [16]You said, 'No, we will flee on horses.' Therefore you will flee! You said, 'We will ride off on swift horses.' Therefore your pursuers will be swift! [17]A thousand will flee at the threat of one, at the threat of five you will all flee away, till you are left like a flagstaff on a mountaintop, like a banner on a hill." [18]Yet the LORD longs to be gracious to you, he rises to show you compassion. For the LORD is a God of justice. Blessed are all who wait for him! [19]O people of Zion, who live in

Jerusalem, you will weep no more. How gracious he will be when you cry for help! As soon as he hears, he will answer you. ²⁰*Although the Lord gives you the bread of adversity and the water of affliction, your teachers will be hidden no more; with your own eyes you will see them.* ²¹*Whether you turn to the right or to the left, your ears will hear a voice behind you, saying, "This is the way; walk in it."* ²²*Then you will defile your idols overlaid with silver and your images covered with gold; you will throw them away like a menstrual cloth and say to them, "Away with you!"* ²³ *He will also send you rain for the seed you sow in the ground, and the food that comes from the land will be rich and plentiful. In that day your cattle will graze in broad meadows.* ²⁴*The oxen and donkeys that work the soil will eat fodder and mash, spread out with fork and shovel.* ²⁵*In the day of great slaughter, when the towers fall, streams of water will flow on every high mountain and every lofty hill.* ²⁶*The moon will shine like the sun, and the sunlight will be seven times brighter, like the light of seven full days, when the LORD binds up the bruises of his people and heals the wounds he inflicted.* ²⁷*See, the Name of the LORD comes from afar, with burning anger and dense clouds of smoke; his lips are full of wrath, and his tongue is a consuming fire.* ²⁸ *His breath is like a rushing torrent, rising up to the neck. He shakes the nations in the sieve of destruction; he places in the jaws of the peoples a bit that leads them astray.* ²⁹*And you will sing as on the night you celebrate a holy festival; your hearts will rejoice as when people go up with flutes to the mountain of the LORD, to the Rock of Israel.* ³⁰*The LORD will cause men to hear his majestic voice and will make them see his arm coming down with raging anger and consuming fire, with cloudburst, thunderstorm and hail.* ³¹*The voice of the LORD will shatter Assyria; with his scepter he will strike them down.* ³²*Every stroke the LORD lays on them with his punishing rod will be to the music of tambourines and harps, as he fights them in battle with the blows of his arm.* ³³*Topheth has long been prepared; it has been made ready or the king. Its fire pit has been made deep and wide, with an abundance of fire and wood; the breath of the LORD, like a stream of burning sulfur, sets it ablaze.*

We live in a world where everybody wants everything right now. At stoplights, you see cars inching up to the line because they are too impatient to wait for the light to turn green. Most times, our impatience gets the best of us. Our impatience has probably also caused us to make bad choices and disastrous decisions.

Wait on God, it will be well worth the wait. Blessed things come to those who wait.

I've Been Changed

Psalm 145 (New International Version)
A psalm of praise. Of David.

¹I will exalt you, my God the King; I will praise your name for ever and ever. ²Every day I will praise you and extol your name for ever and ever. ³Great is the LORD and most worthy of praise; his greatness no one can fathom. ⁴ One generation will commend your works to another; they will tell of your mighty acts. ⁵ They will speak of the glorious splendor of your majesty, and I will meditate on your wonderful works. ⁶They will tell of the power of your awesome works, and I will proclaim your great deeds. ⁷They will celebrate your abundant goodness and joyfully sing of your righteousness. ⁸ The LORD is gracious and compassionate, slow to anger and rich in love. ⁹The LORD is good to all; he has compassion on all he has made. ¹⁰All you have made will praise you, O LORD; your saints will extol you. ¹¹They will tell of the glory of your kingdom and speak of your might, ¹²so that all men may know of your mighty acts and the glorious splendor of your kingdom. ¹³Your kingdom is an everlasting kingdom, and your dominion endures through all generations. The LORD is faithful to all his promises and loving toward all he has made. ¹⁴The LORD upholds all those who fall and lifts up all who are bowed down. ¹⁵The eyes of all look to you, and you give them their food at the proper time. ¹⁶You open your hand and satisfy the desires of every living thing. ¹⁷The LORD is righteous in all his ways and loving toward all he has made. ¹⁸The LORD is near to all who call on him, to all who call on him in truth. ¹⁹He fulfills the desires of those who fear him; he hears their cry and saves them. ²⁰The LORD watches over all who love him, but all the wicked he will destroy. ²¹ My mouth will speak in praise of the LORD. Let every creature praise his holy name for ever and ever.

Change is not easy but it is effective. Sometimes we get sucked into the pressure of trying to be perfect. When we have moments where we are less than perfect, we have a tendency to beat ourselves up. The next time you are having one of those less than worthy moments, look back and see how far you have come from who you used to be. Spend all day today thanking God for the change that has taken place in your life. I know you may not be where you want to be, but celebrate the little steps you have taken to become better.

You must crawl before you can walk and you must walk before you can run. Celebrate the stages of your growth. In life, very little stays the same. Maybe it is time you changed also. Be encouraged. Change is a process, not an event. Celebrate how far you have come. Change is good for you and those around you. Change something today!

❧ ❧ ❧ ❧ ❧ ❧ ❧ ❧ ❧ ❧ ❧ ❧ ❧ ❧ ❧ ❧

Guard Your Heart

Proverbs 4:23-27 (New International Version)
23 Above all else, guard your heart, for it is the wellspring of life. 24 Put away perversity from your mouth; keep corrupt talk far from your lips. 25 Let your eyes look straight ahead, fix your gaze directly before you. 26 Make level paths for your feet and take only ways that are firm. 27 Do not swerve to the right or the left; keep your foot from evil.

The most precious thing that any of us possess is not our money, houses or cars. Our most prized possession is our heart. It is hard to bounce back from heartbreak. You can break your arm and it may take weeks to heal. You can break your leg and it make take months to heal. A broken heart may take a lifetime to heal. Don't leave yourself open too quickly to others because your vulnerability could lead you to becoming your enemies' next victim. They would love nothing more than to tear your heart out and crush your spirit. Some people try to get close to you so they can discover how to break you.

Many of us can survive taking a hit almost anywhere on our bodies except the heart. There is something deadly and dangerous about being hit in the heart. Be very careful of who you allow to have your heart because sometimes, they are the very ones who will snatch it out and destroy you.

When demonic intruders are getting too close to your heart, your spiritual radars must alert you that they have gotten too close. The only people in this season with access to your heart should be those individuals who have your best interests at heart. Your heart is too precious to leave it unprotected.

Under Distress

James 1:12-15 (New International Version)
¹²Blessed is the man who perseveres under trial, because when he has stood the test, he will receive the crown of life that God has promised to those who love him. ¹³When tempted, no one should say, "God is tempting me." For God cannot be tempted by evil, nor does he tempt anyone; ¹⁴but each one is tempted when, by his own evil desire, he is dragged away and enticed. ¹⁵Then, after desire has conceived, it gives birth to sin; and sin, when it is full-grown, gives birth to death.

As you are traveling along the highway, you can always find a vehicle that is pulled over with hazard lights flashing as a signal of distress. As we go through life, there are times that we are under distress. There are different levels of stress such as financial distress, emotional distress and even physical distress. When you're in stressful situations, here are a few spiritual power points to help you through.
1. Pray and persevere.
2. Pray and don't panic.
3. Pray and be patient.

If you are going to pray then don't worry. If you are going to worry, don't pray.

The Troubles of This World

John 14:1-3 (New International Version)
Jesus Comforts His Disciples

¹Do not let your hearts be troubled. Trust in God; trust also in me. ²In my Father's house are many rooms; if it were not so, I would have told you. I am going there to prepare a place for you. ³And if I go and prepare a place for you, I will come back and take you to be with me that you also may be where I am.

Life has a unique way of throwing us unexpected curves. One minute you are on top of the world and the next day you are fighting your way out of the basement. For some of us, life can be filled with one trouble after another. So what do you do when you're faced with the troubles of this world?

1. Don't worry about the things of this world. They will eventually fade away.
2. Recognize God is preparing something great for you. This is not all there is to life. God has more in store for you.
3. Remember that the "stuff" that matters down here won't matter up there!

Trouble don't last always.

What Gets God Excited

Psalm 100 (New International Version)
A Psalm. for giving thanks.
¹ Shout for joy to the LORD, all the earth. ² Worship the LORD with gladness; come before him with joyful songs. ³ Know that the LORD is God. It is he who made us, and we are his we are his people, the sheep of his pasture. ⁴ Enter his gates with thanksgiving and his courts with praise; give thanks to him and praise his name. ⁵ For the LORD is good and his love endures forever; his faithfulness continues through all generations.

Many of us go through life looking and expecting others to make us happy. When was the last time you rolled out of the bed determined to make God excited? How can we bring a smile to God's face?

Start by realizing that God loves noise. God gets excited when we make noise for Him. Verse 1 of Psalm 100 says "shout for joy". No matter what the weather may be, no matter how you feel about what you have to do – SHOUT! Whatever you're doing right now, I guarantee you if you can find a place to let loose, a shout will make you feel better.

God gets excited simply because you know who He is to you. Take a second and just think about who God is to you and watch something get ready to break in your life.

Remember why God woke you up today. When you take into account that out of all the people God could have chosen not to wake up, God took the time to make sure you were breathing. He instructs those of us who have breath to give Him the praise. Guess what? God created us to be praisers. Send your praise up to get whatever you need today.

Now

Hebrews 11:1 (New International Version)
By Faith
¹Now faith is being sure of what we hope for and certain of what we do not see.

So often when we talk about God, we usually refer to what God is going to do or what he is getting ready to do. Sometimes in our own lives, we delay the blessings of God because we don't operate with a "right now faith". Hebrews 11:1 points to the reality that faith is an issue of "now". It reads "now faith is". Therefore, those things we are hoping for as well as praying for we should believe it for now. Don't put off tomorrow what you can believe God for today.

- Your breakthrough is now.
- Your miracle is happening now.
- Your healing is occurring now.
- Your prayers are being answered now.

Expect big things today.

ShadowBoxing

James 4:1-4 (New International Version)
Submit Yourselves to God

¹What causes fights and quarrels among you? Don't they come from your desires that battle within you? ²You want something but don't get it. You kill and covet, but you cannot have what you want. You quarrel and fight. You do not have, because you do not ask God. ³When you ask, you do not receive, because you ask with wrong motives, that you may spend what you get on your pleasures. ⁴You adulterous people, don't you know that friendship with the world is hatred toward God? Anyone who chooses to be a friend of the world becomes an enemy of God.

I have met several people who have a battle everyday as soon as their feet hit the ground. They feel like it is so hard to do good but trouble is so easy to find. Maybe you are one of those individuals who do not have to look for trouble, it just comes looking for you. In moments like these, it is so easy to blame everybody other than yourself for what you're going through. However, could it be that the person you are really at war with is you? Sometimes our biggest enemy lives inside of us. Free yourself from yourself today.

The fight is fixed. God is on your side.

Be True To You

John 8:28-32 (New International Version)

28 So Jesus said, "When you have lifted up the Son of Man, then you will know that I am the one I claim to be and that I do nothing on my own but speak just what the Father has taught me. 29 The one who sent me is with me; he has not left me alone, for I always do what pleases him." 30 Even as he spoke, many put their faith in him.

The Children of Abraham

31 To the Jews who had believed him, Jesus said, "If you hold to my teaching, you are really my disciples. 32 Then you will know the truth, and the truth will set you free."

During Halloween, many people go out and purchase costumes in order to dress up and look like somebody different. The problem I have is so many of us are wearing so many different masks, we have forgotten who we really are. We have a mask for work, a mask for church, a mask for family and a mask for friends. With so many masks, we run the risk of forgetting which mask to put on for which occasion. Don't deny yourself the awesome blessing of authenticity. To be at this place does three powerful things for you.

- It releases you to be free from the expectation of others.
- It releases you to be secure in who you are.
- It releases you to be at peace because you have nothing to prove.

There is nothing more frustrating than being a people pleaser. Regardless of what others do, be true to you.

Constructive Criticism

Proverbs 12:1-2 (New International Version)
¹ Whoever loves discipline loves knowledge, but he who hates correction is stupid. ² A good man obtains favor from the LORD, but the LORD condemns a crafty man.

As a Resident Chaplain, each week I spend a day in clinical supervision. This is an opportunity for me to receive feedback on my work and research. When I first began, I was most worried about the opinions of others. Whenever there was a response to something I said, I automatically became emotionally defensive.

Many of us make the tragic mistake of wearing our feelings on our sleeve. As a result, our feelings get exposed to unhealthy stuff that has the potential to damage us. Criticism is not always bad because we are not always giving our best. All criticism is not good but at the same time it is not all bad. Internalize what is good or what you can use. Get rid of criticism that is destructive and embrace the constructive ideas. I look at taking criticism like a savoring good fish. Eat the meat and throw away the bones.

I'm Desperate for God

Psalm 63 (New International Version)

¹ O God, you are my God, earnestly I seek you; my soul thirsts for you, my body longs for you, in a dry and weary land where there is no water. ² I have seen you in the sanctuary and beheld your power and your glory. ³ Because your love is better than life, my lips will glorify you. ⁴ I will praise you as long as I live, and in your name I will lift up my hands. ⁵ My soul will be satisfied as with the richest of foods; with singing lips my mouth will praise you. ⁶ On my bed I remember you; I think of you through the watches of the night. ⁷ Because you are my help, I sing in the shadow of your wings. ⁸ My soul clings to you; your right hand upholds me. ⁹ They who seek my life will be destroyed; they will go down to the depths of the earth. ¹⁰ They will be given over to the sword and become food for jackals. ¹¹ But the king will rejoice in God; all who swear by God's name will praise him, while the mouths of liars will be silenced.

We live in a world where so many of us are chasing after stuff that won't last. There is nothing wrong with being desperate. Just make sure you are desperate for the right stuff and the right person.

Remember that all things will eventually break down and people will eventually let you down but God is always around. He is omnipresent. Be desperate for God. Be dedicated to the task at hand. Be determined not to let anything slow you down.

Today I pray that you become so desperate for God that your every thought is about Him. Let nothing upset you, bother you, worry you, frustrate you, distract you or stress you today. Remind yourself that you are "too desperate to be denied".
Desperation leads to celebration.
Desperation leads to liberation.
Desperation leads to promotion.

Be too desperate to be denied.

Rev. Dr. James E. Jones, Jr.

I'm In Over My Head

Psalm 69 (New International Version)

¹Save me, O God, for the waters have come up to my neck. ²I sink in the miry depths, where there is no foothold. I have come into the deep waters; the floods engulf me. ³I am worn out calling for help; my throat is parched. My eyes fail, looking for my God. ⁴Those who hate me without reason outnumber the hairs of my head; many are my enemies without cause, those who seek to destroy me. I am forced to restore what I did not steal. ⁵You know my folly, O God; my guilt is not hidden from you. ⁶May those who hope in you not be disgraced because of me, O Lord, the LORD Almighty; may those who seek you not be put to shame because of me, O God of Israel. ⁷For I endure scorn for your sake, and shame covers my face. ⁸I am a stranger to my brothers, an alien to my own mother's sons; ⁹for zeal for your house consumes me, and the insults of those who insult you fall on me. ¹⁰When I weep and fast, I must endure scorn; ¹¹when I put on sackcloth, people make sport of me. ¹²Those who sit at the gate mock me, and I am the song of the drunkards. ¹³But I pray to you, O LORD, in the time of your favor; in your great love, O God, answer me with your sure salvation. ¹⁴Rescue me from the mire, do not let me sink; deliver me from those who hate me, from the deep waters. ¹⁵Do not let the floodwaters engulf me or the depths swallow me up or the pit close its mouth over me. ¹⁶Answer me, O LORD, out of the goodness of your love; in your great mercy turn to me. ¹⁷Do not hide your face from your servant; answer me quickly, for I am in trouble. ¹⁸ Come near and rescue me; redeem me because of my foes. ¹⁹You know how I am scorned, disgraced and shamed; all my enemies are before you. ²⁰Scorn has broken my heart and has left me helpless; I looked for sympathy, but there was none, for comforters, but I found none. ²¹They put gall in my food and gave me vinegar for my thirst. ²²May the table set before them become a snare; may it become retribution and a trap. ²³May their eyes be darkened so they cannot see, and their backs be bent forever. ²⁴Pour out your wrath on them; let your fierce anger overtake them. ²⁵May their place be deserted; let there be no one to dwell in their tents. ²⁶For they persecute those you wound and talk about the pain of those you hurt. ²⁷ Charge them with crime upon crime; do not let them share in your salvation. ²⁸May they be blotted out of the book of life and not be listed with the righteous. ²⁹I am in pain and distress; may your salvation, O God, protect me.³⁰I will praise

God's name in song and glorify him with thanksgiving. ³¹This will please the LORD more than an ox, more than a bull with its horns and hoofs. ³²The poor will see and be glad—you who seek God, may your hearts live! ³³The LORD hears the needy and does not despise his captive people. ³⁴ Let heaven and earth praise him, the seas and all that move in them, ³⁵for God will save Zion and rebuild the cities of Judah. Then people will settle there and possess it; ³⁶the children of his servants will inherit it, and those who love his name will dwell there.

Have you ever felt overworked, overwhelmed or just overextended? Life gets tough even for the best of us. The pressures of this world can wear you down. Everybody needs something from you and everybody is expecting something out of you. No matter how strong you are or how good you are, life can surely get too tough for one person to handle. Sometimes you just feel like you are in over your head.

Three spiritual strategies for the next time you are feeling this way:
1. Recognize what you're up against. Usually, when a soldier is preparing for war, they study their opponent. Study your opponent's every move in order for you to be prepared when the battle comes.
2. Remember to always have confidence in God. There are times when you must remind yourself that God has not brought you this far to leave you.
3. Realize that in spite of your pain, you can still release a praise. Your praise cannot be contingent upon your pain or your circumstance. As a matter of fact, our pain should push out an even greater praise. The greater the pain, the greater your praise should be.

I Almost Walked Away From God

Psalm 73 (New International Version)
A Psalm of Asaph.

¹Surely God is good to Israel, to those who are pure in heart. ²But as for me, my feet had almost slipped; I had nearly lost my foothold. ³For I envied the arrogant when I saw the prosperity of the wicked. ⁴ They have no struggles; their bodies are healthy and strong. ⁵ They are free from the burdens common to man; they are not plagued by human ills. ⁶ Therefore pride is their necklace; they clothe themselves with violence. ⁷ From their callous hearts comes iniquity the evil conceits of their minds know no limits. ⁸ They scoff, and speak with malice; in their arrogance they threaten oppression. ⁹ Their mouths lay claim to heaven, and their tongues take possession of the earth. ¹⁰ Therefore their people turn to them and drink up waters in abundance. ¹¹ They say, "How can God know? Does the Most High have knowledge?" ¹² This is what the wicked are like— always carefree, they increase in wealth. ¹³ Surely in vain have I kept my heart pure; in vain have I washed my hands in innocence. ¹⁴ All day long I have been plagued; I have been punished every morning. ¹⁵ If I had said, "I will speak thus," I would have betrayed your children.

¹⁶ When I tried to understand all this, it was oppressive to me ¹⁷ till I entered the sanctuary of God; then I understood their final destiny. ¹⁸ Surely you place them on slippery ground; you cast them down to ruin. ¹⁹ How suddenly are they destroyed, completely swept away by terrors! ²⁰ As a dream when one awakes, so when you arise, O Lord, you will despise them as fantasies. ²¹ When my heart was grieved and my spirit embittered, ²² I was senseless and ignorant; I was a brute beast before you. ²³ Yet I am always with you; you hold me by my right hand. ²⁴ You guide me with your counsel, and afterward you will take me into glory. ²⁵ Whom have I in heaven but you? And earth has nothing I desire besides you. ²⁶ My flesh and my heart may fail, but God is the strength of my heart and my portion forever. ²⁷ Those who are far from you will perish; you destroy all who are unfaithful to you. ²⁸ But as for me, it is good to be near God. I have made the Sovereign LORD my refuge; I will tell of all your deeds.

During some of my most difficult personal struggles, I seemed to be at war with much in my life. My personal life was strained, my friends were unavailable due to their own personal challenges, and the church had severely wounded me. It was while I was in this dark place that walking away from everything seemed to make more sense than trying to fight any longer. During this season, I almost walked away from God. Just as the thought crossed my mind, God spoke to me and said, "When life is good, you take the credit. When life is bad, you blame God."

Before you walk away from God, remember God has been walking with you every step of the way. You've come too far to give up now. Before you walk away from Him, walk away from "it" because "it" is not worth losing Him.

Rev. Dr. James E. Jones, Jr.

God Always Comes Through

Psalm 102:1-17 (New International Version)

¹ Hear my prayer, O LORD; let my cry for help come to you. ² Do not hide your face from me when I am in distress. Turn your ear to me; when I call, answer me quickly. ³ For my days vanish like smoke; my bones burn like glowing embers. ⁴ My heart is blighted and withered like grass; I forget to eat my food. ⁵ Because of my loud groaning I am reduced to skin and bones. ⁶ I am like a desert owl, like an owl among the ruins. ⁷ I lie awake; I have become like a bird alone on a roof. ⁸ All day long my enemies taunt me; those who rail against me use my name as a curse. ⁹ For I eat ashes as my food and mingle my drink with tears ¹⁰ because of your great wrath, for you have taken me up and thrown me aside. ¹¹ My days are like the evening shadow; I wither away like grass. ¹² But you, O LORD, sit enthroned forever; your renown endures through all generations. ¹³ You will arise and have compassion on Zion, for it is time to show favor to her; the appointed time has come. ¹⁴ For her stones are dear to your servants; her very dust moves them to pity. ¹⁵ The nations will fear the name of the LORD, all the kings of the earth will revere your glory. ¹⁶ For the LORD will rebuild Zion and appear in his glory. ¹⁷ He will respond to the prayer of the destitute; he will not despise their plea.

There are moments in life where things can look pretty hopeless. It may feel like one of those seasons where you wonder if it will ever stop raining. Family has turned their back on you and friends are doing more walking out of your life than walking in. Whatever the situation may be, remember that God is always on time. He loves you enough to make a special delivery just for you. God always comes through.

Just remember, He will see you through.

Remember Me

Psalm 25:1-12 (New International Version)

¹To you, O LORD, I lift up my soul; ² in you I trust, O my God. Do not let me be put to shame, nor let my enemies triumph over me. ³ No one whose hope is in you will ever be put to shame, but they will be put to shame who are treacherous without excuse. ⁴ Show me your ways, O LORD, teach me your paths; ⁵ guide me in your truth and teach me, for you are God my Savior, and my hope is in you all day long. ⁶ Remember, O LORD, your great mercy and love, for they are from of old. ⁷ Remember not the sins of my youth and my rebellious ways; according to your love remember me, for you are good, O LORD. ⁸ Good and upright is the LORD; therefore he instructs sinners in his ways. ⁹ He guides the humble in what is right and teaches them his way. ¹⁰ All the ways of the LORD are loving and faithful for those who keep the demands of his covenant. ¹¹ For the sake of your name, O LORD, forgive my iniquity, though it is great. ¹² Who, then, is the man that fears the LORD ? He will instruct him in the way chosen for him.

Even though we are sinners by nature and constantly stand in need of forgiveness, it is a privilege to ask God to remember you. Maybe you have gone through experiences where somebody close to you forgot a date that was important to you. Don't take it so personal when others around you don't remember what matters to you. I have found strength in knowing that God never forgets us and is always available. It doesn't matter if its day or night, rain or shine when you call on God. He will answer. If today is a day where you don't feel like pushing, push anyway.

God has not forgotten you.

Rev. Dr. James E. Jones, Jr.

He Gave Us All He Had

John 3:10-16 (New International Version)

¹⁰"You are Israel's teacher," said Jesus, "and do you not understand these things? ¹¹I tell you the truth, we speak of what we know, and we testify to what we have seen, but still you people do not accept our testimony. ¹²I have spoken to you of earthly things and you do not believe; how then will you believe if I speak of heavenly things? ¹³No one has ever gone into heaven except the one who came from heaven—the Son of Man. ¹⁴Just as Moses lifted up the snake in the desert, so the Son of Man must be lifted up, ¹⁵that everyone who believes in him may have eternal life. ¹⁶"For God so loved the world that he gave his one and only Son,[c] that whoever believes in him shall not perish but have eternal life.

It is hard for some people to express how they feel. They find themselves trapped within their own pain or even paralyzed by the events of the past. They are never able to fully release themselves to experience the calming presence of a God who can handle our failure just as much as he can handle our success. God demonstrated the power and the freedom of being able to release because He gave up everything He had for us.

God gave you all He had. Now He is waiting on us to give Him everything we have. Live each day as if it is your last. Tomorrow is not promised. Live to love and love to live.

Walk In Freedom

Psalm 119:45-50 (New International Version)

[45] *I will walk about in freedom, for I have sought out your precepts.* [46] *I will speak of your statutes before kings and will not be put to shame,* [47] *for I delight in your commands because I love them.* [48] *I lift up my hands to your commands, which I love, and I meditate on your decrees. z Zayin* [49] *Remember your word to your servant, for you have given me hope.* [50] *My comfort in my suffering is this: Your promise preserves my life.*

I have spent much of my life living out the expectations of others while allowing them to place their limitations on me. Both of these realities left me empty and frustrated. God desires you to live in a place of freedom. While we have clear boundaries spiritually, far too many of us have placed boundaries on our feelings. This week, give yourself space to move around. Give yourself space to:

- Make mistakes. It's okay not to be perfect.
- Make moves. Don't stay where you are because you have to but because you want to.
- Make memories. You can't remember what you have not experienced.

Give yourself and those in your life, including God, some more room to move around in. Walk in the freedom of Jesus. Freedom is priceless.

The Bigger They Are...The Harder They Fall

2 Thessalonians 1 (New International Version)
¹Paul, Silas and Timothy, To the church of the Thessalonians in God our Father and the Lord Jesus Christ:
²Grace and peace to you from God the Father and the Lord Jesus Christ. ³We ought always to thank God for you, brothers, and rightly so, because your faith is growing more and more, and the love every one of you has for each other is increasing. ⁴Therefore, among God's churches we boast about your perseverance and faith in all the persecutions and trials you are enduring. ⁵All this is evidence that God's judgment is right, and as a result you will be counted worthy of the kingdom of God, for which you are suffering. ⁶God is just: He will pay back trouble to those who trouble you ⁷and give relief to you who are troubled, and to us as well. This will happen when the Lord Jesus is revealed from heaven in blazing fire with his powerful angels. ⁸He will punish those who do not know God and do not obey the gospel of our Lord Jesus. ⁹They will be punished with everlasting destruction and shut out from the presence of the Lord and from the majesty of his power ¹⁰on the day he comes to be glorified in his holy people and to be marveled at among all those who have believed. This includes you, because you believed our testimony to you. ¹¹With this in mind, we constantly pray for you, that our God may count you worthy of his calling, and that by his power he may fulfill every good purpose of yours and every act prompted by your faith. ¹²We pray this so that the name of our Lord Jesus may be glorified in you, and you in him, according to the grace of our God and the Lord Jesus Christ.

You may be facing some big situation and even bigger problems. You may be losing your job, losing a loved one or going through a divorce. You may be confronted with paying bills that you have no money to pay. You may be preparing to take a major test or additional training at your job in order to get a promotion. All of these circumstances are BIG to somebody today. What may be a small problem to you could actually be a BIG problem to someone else.

Don't be intimidated by giant size situations. God does some of his best work when the situation appears to be bigger than us. Big situations just give God more room to bless you. God is bigger than you think and so are you. Think big.

43

Rev. Dr. James E. Jones, Jr.

It's In Him

Acts 17:26-27 (New International Version)
²⁶From one man he made every nation of men, that they should inhabit the whole earth; and he determined the times set for them and the exact places where they should live. ²⁷God did this so that men would seek him and perhaps reach out for him and find him, though he is not far from each one of us.

Everything that is, God created it. Without the presence of God, nothing exists. In Him, we discover life and its meaning. In Him, we realize that our very movement is a gift from Him. Our being is predicated upon God's desire to be. We are who we are because God is who He is. Don't tolerate life but celebrate it because it is a gift from God. As you go throughout this day, learn how to flow in Him and take it one day at a time.

Celebrate creations and the Creator.

The Blessing of Being Broke

Luke 6:20-26 (New International Version)

²⁰Looking at his disciples, he said: "Blessed are you who *are poor, for yours is the kingdom of God. ²¹Blessed are you who hunger now, for you will be satisfied. Blessed are you who weep now, for you will laugh. ²²Blessed are you when men hate you, when they exclude you and insult you and reject your name as evil, because of the Son of Man. ²³"Rejoice in that day and leap for joy, because great is your reward in heaven. For that is how their fathers treated the prophets. ²⁴"But woe to you who are rich, for you have already received your comfort. ²⁵Woe to you who are well fed now, for you will go hungry. Woe to you who laugh now, for you will mourn and weep. ²⁶Woe to you when all men speak well of you, for that is how their fathers treated the false prophets.*

Blessings and being broke are not contradictions but actually a bridge that could lead to celebration. Anybody can praise Him when things are good, but can you praise Him when there is nothing to shout about? An authentic worship is released when there is nothing to gain and everything to lose. When you are at the point of desperation and the only constant in your life is God, trust him exclusively for a way out of the situation. It doesn't matter if you are emotionally broke, physically broke, spiritually broke or financially broke. Worship God for who he is and watch things start turning around. Our praise moves the hand of God but our worship moves the heart of God.

Rev. Dr. James E. Jones, Jr.

No Other Name

Philippians 2:1-10 (New International Version)
Imitating Christ's Humility

¹If you have any encouragement from being united with Christ, if any comfort from his love, if any fellowship with the Spirit, if any tenderness and compassion, ²then make my joy complete by being like-minded, having the same love, being one in spirit and purpose. ³Do nothing out of selfish ambition or vain conceit, but in humility consider others better than yourselves. ⁴Each of you should look not only to your own interests, but also to the interests of others. ⁵Your attitude should be the same as that of Christ Jesus: ⁶Who, being in very nature[a] God, did not consider equality with God something to be grasped, ⁷but made himself nothing, taking the very nature[b] of a servant, being made in human likeness. ⁸And being found in appearance as a man, he humbled himself and became obedient to death— even death on a cross! ⁹Therefore God exalted him to the highest place and gave him the name that is above every name, ¹⁰that at the name of Jesus every knee should bow, in heaven and on earth and under the earth,

I am not very good with names. I will remember a face but quickly forget a name. Historically, we took pride in our names but now when someone doesn't like their name, they simply change it. One name that has not changed is the name of Jesus. His name is still the most powerful name you should know. No other name can save you. No other name can change your situation while you are still in your situation. There is no name on earth like the name of Jesus.

Say His name! Say His name!

You Can Do It

Joshua 1:7-9 (New International Version)

⁷ Be strong and very courageous. Be careful to obey all the law my servant Moses gave you; do not turn from it to the right or to the left, that you may be successful wherever you go. ⁸ Do not let this Book of the Law depart from your mouth; meditate on it day and night, so that you may be careful to do everything written in it. Then you will be prosperous and successful. ⁹ Have I not commanded you? Be strong and courageous. Do not be terrified; do not be discouraged, for the LORD your God will be with you wherever you go."

Have you ever been told you weren't good enough? Have you ever been told you will never accomplish anything? Have you ever been told you weren't smart enough? If you answered yes to any of these questions, then this word is for you. You can do it. What can you do? You can do whatever God has purposed. God created you with a specific purpose. You were not created to be or to live in failure. No matter how many times failure has crept into your mind or existence, you are not a failure. You can do all things Christ which gives you strength daily. Throughout this day, speak "I can" over every situation in your life. Remove the word can't from your vocabulary.

Only What You Do For Christ Will Last

Psalm 127 (New International Version)
¹ Unless the LORD builds the house, its builders labor in vain. Unless the LORD watches over the city, the watchmen stand guard in vain. ² In vain you rise early and stay up late, toiling for food to eat - for He grants sleep to those he loves. ³ Sons are a heritage from the LORD, children a reward from him. ⁴ Like arrows in the hands of a warrior are sons born in one's youth. ⁵ Blessed is the man whose quiver is full of them. They will not be put to shame when they contend with their enemies in the gate.

Many of us spend so much time trying to "become". We get to work early and we leave late, at times at the expense of our own families. We spend our lifetime looking for significance only to discover it when we arrive at the end of life's journey. I pray that you make the ultimate discovery that all is vanity and only what you do for Christ will last. Living for Christ makes life worth living.

Return to Sender

Isaiah 55:11 (New International Version)
¹¹ so is my word that goes out from my mouth: It will not return to me empty, but will accomplish what I desire and achieve the purpose for which I sent it.

There is power in what you say. Life or death is in your mouth. We live in a world that does not place a great deal of value on someone's word because it is easy to go back on it. Let me take this moment to empower you that when God delivers a "word", it never comes back without accomplishing its purpose. Unlike the mail system or emails, you don't ever have to worry about God's work returning to sender without fulfilling His purpose.

No Other Choice

Proverbs 3:5 (New International Version)
⁵ Trust in the LORD with all your heart and lean not on your own understanding;

Trust is a serious word. If you have to preface your statement to another individual by saying "don't tell anyone" or "this is just between us", then chances are good that person can't be trusted. Remember this: trust is not something that should be given. It must be earned.

Some of my greatest pain has come from the lips of those I trusted so dearly. Be careful who you label trustworthy. I have discovered in life that there are no permanent friends and no permanent enemies. You can trust God with anything when other people and systems have let you down. You can always depend on God. You have no other choice but to trust Him.

A High Cost to Low Living

Romans 3:23 (New International Version)
²³for all have sinned and fall short of the glory of God,

Sin comes in all different shapes and sizes. It has the ability to look, feel or smell very appealing. However, sin is dangerous and the results of it can be quite costly. Have you ever noticed that the price of sin keeps increasing? More and more people are finding themselves facing some difficult situations all because of sin. Remember that for every choice we make, there is a consequence. The price of sin is not worth the pleasure. Try to walk by the spirit today, you will feel better.

Living in the Overflow

Romans 15:12-13 (New International Version)

¹²And again, Isaiah says, "The Root of Jesse will spring up, one who will arise to rule over the nations; the Gentiles will hope in him." ¹³May the God of hope fill you with all joy and peace as you trust in him, so that you may overflow with hope by the power of the Holy Spirit.

Are you tired of living from paycheck to paycheck and never having any extra? God's desire for you life is for you to be a success. God has promised to supply all of your needs and its God's desire to bless you so much that you are able to be generous on every occasion. You've been surviving long enough. Now it is time to start thriving. As we walk in obedience with God, He has promised to bless everything around us. Today, start speaking abundance over your situation.

Build Me Up – Don't Tear Me Down

Romans 15:1-5 (New International Version)

¹We who are strong ought to bear with the failings of the weak and not to please ourselves. ²Each of us should please his neighbor for his good, to build him up. ³For even Christ did not please himself but, as it is written: "The insults of those who insult you have fallen on me." ⁴For everything that was written in the past was written to teach us, so that through endurance and the encouragement of the Scriptures we might have hope. ⁵May the God who gives endurance and encouragement give you a spirit of unity among yourselves as you follow Christ Jesus,

The world is filled with people who make others feel small in order for them to feel bigger. It's easy to stand with someone when things are going good but the test of any friendship is whether friends will stand with you when things are falling apart. Usually it is easier to kick a person when they are already down. A real friend will concentrate on building you up and not tearing you down. Be patient with those around you and remember that God is not through with them or you yet.

What Have You Done For Me Lately?

Psalm 107:1-9 (New International Version)

¹ Give thanks to the LORD, for he is good; his love endures forever. ² Let the redeemed of the LORD say this— those he redeemed from the hand of the foe, ³those he gathered from the lands, from east and west, from north and south. ⁴ Some wandered in desert wastelands, finding no way to a city where they could settle. ⁵ They were hungry and thirsty, and their lives ebbed away. ⁶ Then they cried out to the LORD in their trouble, and he delivered them from their distress. ⁷ He led them by a straight way to a city where they could settle. ⁸ Let them give thanks to the LORD for his unfailing love and his wonderful deeds for men, ⁹ for he satisfies the thirsty and fills the hungry with good things.

Each and every day I meet somebody who is extremely unhappy with their lives and critical about everything. These types of people are usually never satisfied. Why is it that the unhappiest people are usually the loudest? Let's change all of that now. Today, you say something. If God has done anything for you lately, then you should not mind saying something to someone about how good God has been and all He has done for you. Say something.

Which Road?

Proverbs 3:5-6 (New International Version)
⁵ Trust in the LORD with all your heart and lean not on your own understanding; ⁶ in all your ways acknowledge him, and he will make your paths straight.

Life will take us down many different roads. Today I want to share with you the 5 most popular roads we travel:

1. The Road of Promise – This is the road we are on from birth. Your potential is birthed out of your promise. We all start out with promising futures.
2. The Road of Purpose – Unlike the Road of Promise where we are born in our potential, on the Road of Purpose, we discover it as we make the journey. The Road of Purpose is the road where you discover why you are here.
3. The Road of Pain – This is the hardest road because it is bumpy, dark and difficult to travel on. It is filled with bad choices, bad decisions, negative influences and moments you wish you could take back.
4. The Road of Peace – This is the road you run into after you've come through pain. The Road of Peace is a place in life where things may not be perfect but they are smooth enough for you to get through them.
5. The Road of Prosperity – This is the road of enjoyment and fulfillment. This road leads to a place where you don't worry about anything or want for anything. The place of prosperity is not about what you have, but where you are. It's about being content in all circumstances.

At this very moment, which road are you traveling on?

A Praise Party

Psalm 150 (New International Version)
¹ Praise the LORD. Praise God in his sanctuary; praise him in his mighty heavens. ² Praise him for his acts of power; praise him for his surpassing greatness. ³ Praise him with the sounding of the trumpet, praise him with the harp and lyre, ⁴ praise him with tambourine and dancing, praise him with the strings and flute, ⁵ praise him with the clash of cymbals, praise him with resounding cymbals. ⁶ Let everything that has breath praise the LORD. Praise the LORD.

I don't know too many people who don't enjoy a good celebration. Whether it is a retirement celebration, wedding celebration, holiday celebration, birthday celebration or an anniversary celebration, many of us love to celebrate. Today I invite you to join me in an exclusive celebration. Who are we celebrating? God! Why are we celebrating? Because of all He has done for us. Let's look at what has God done for you lately:

- God has fed you
- God has protected you
- God has provided for you
- God has clothed you
- God has healed you
- God has kept you
- God has rescued you
- God has forgiven you
- God has blessed you
- God still loves you.

With that in mind, let the celebration begin every day! You are alive and this is cause for a celebration. You do not have to wait for a special occasion or invitation. I invite you to find something to celebrate. When you praise Him, you feel better.

No Limits

John 15:1-13 (New International Version)
The Vine and the Branches

¹"I am the true vine, and my Father is the gardener. ²He cuts off every branch in me that bears no fruit, while every branch that does bear fruit he prunes so that it will be even more fruitful. ³You are already clean because of the word I have spoken to you. ⁴Remain in me, and I will remain in you. No branch can bear fruit by itself; it must remain in the vine. Neither can you bear fruit unless you remain in me. ⁵"I am the vine; you are the branches. If a man remains in me and I in him, he will bear much fruit; apart from me you can do nothing. ⁶If anyone does not remain in me, he is like a branch that is thrown away and withers; such branches are picked up, thrown into the fire and burned. ⁷If you remain in me and my words remain in you, ask whatever you wish, and it will be given you. ⁸This is to my Father's glory, that you bear much fruit, showing yourselves to be my disciples. ⁹"As the Father has loved me, so have I loved you. Now remain in my love. ¹⁰If you obey my commands, you will remain in my love, just as I have obeyed my Father's commands and remain in his love. ¹¹I have told you this so that my joy may be in you and that your joy may be complete. ¹²My command is this: Love each other as I have loved you. ¹³Greater love has no one than this, that he lay down his life for his friends.

Life is about growth, development and opportunities. The problem with many people is sometimes we miss opportunities because we've placed limits on God. This then places limits on us. Take God out of the box and watch God take you to places you never dreamed possible. Don't limit your possibilities by limiting God's potential.

My Pain Won't Go Away

Jeremiah 15:1-18 (New International Version)

¹ Then the LORD said to me: "Even if Moses and Samuel were to stand before me, my heart would not go out to this people. Send them away from my presence! Let them go! ² And if they ask you, 'Where shall we go?' tell them, 'This is what the LORD says: " 'Those destined for death, to death; those for the sword, to the sword; those for starvation, to starvation; those for captivity, to captivity.' ³ "I will send four kinds of destroyers against them," declares the LORD, "the sword to kill and the dogs to drag away and the birds of the air and the beasts of the earth to devour and destroy. ⁴ I will make them abhorrent to all the kingdoms of the earth because of what Manasseh son of Hezekiah king of Judah did in Jerusalem. ⁵ "Who will have pity on you, O Jerusalem? Who will mourn for you? Who will stop to ask how you are? ⁶ You have rejected me," declares the LORD. "You keep on backsliding. So I will lay hands on you and destroy you; I can no longer show compassion. ⁷ I will winnow them with a winnowing fork at the city gates of the land. I will bring bereavement and destruction on my people, for they have not changed their ways. ⁸ I will make their widows more numerous than the sand of the sea. At midday I will bring a destroyer against the mothers of their young men; suddenly I will bring down on them anguish and terror. ⁹ The mother of seven will grow faint and breathe her last. Her sun will set while it is still day; she will be disgraced and humiliated. I will put the survivors to the sword before their enemies," declares the LORD.

¹⁰ Alas, my mother, that you gave me birth, a man with whom the whole land strives and contends! I have neither lent nor borrowed, yet everyone curses me. ¹¹ The LORD said, "Surely I will deliver you for a good purpose; surely I will make your enemies plead with you in times of disaster and times of distress. ¹² "Can a man break iron— iron from the north—or bronze? ¹³ Your wealth and your treasures I will give as plunder, without charge, because of all your sins throughout your country. ¹⁴ I will enslave you to your enemies in a land you do not know, for my anger will kindle a fire that will burn against you." ¹⁵ You understand, O LORD; remember me and care for me. Avenge me on my persecutors. You are long-suffering—do not take me away; think of how I suffer reproach for your sake. ¹⁶ When your words came, I ate them; they were my joy and my heart's delight, for I bear your name, O LORD God Almighty. ¹⁷ I never sat in the company of revelers, never made merry with them; I sat alone because your hand was on me and you had filled me with indignation. ¹⁸ *Why is my pain unending and my wound grievous and incurable? Will you be to me like a deceptive brook, like a spring that fails?*

Ever felt like your pain just would not go away? Day after day, your hurt and problems seem to follow you. Sometimes you feel like crying when you don't even know what's wrong. Other times it is hard pulling yourself out of bed. Maybe you hurt someone or somebody hurt you. Either way, pain is never easy to deal with or to get over. Some pain you learn how to get through and some pain seems to linger forever. Be encouraged because God can take the pain away. Keep pushing because God is the ultimate pain killer.

No Time For Childish Games

1 Corinthians 13:1-2 (New International Version)
Love

¹If I speak in the tongues of men and of angels, but have not love, I am only a resounding gong or a clanging cymbal. ²If I have the gift of prophecy and can fathom all mysteries and all knowledge, and if I have a faith that can move mountains, but have not love, I am nothing.

As children, we love playing games. Whether it was dodge ball, hide and go seek or video games, these moments provided release from a mundane life. However, the season for playing games for certain people has been far removed. It is dangerous to play games with the feelings and emotions of others. It is far more dangerous to play games with God. Don't add God to the list of people you plan on "playing" today. God knows we are not perfect but we owe it to God to keep it real.

Rev. Dr. James E. Jones, Jr.

Watch Out for False Teachers

2 Peter 1:1-8 (New International Version)

¹Simon Peter, a servant and apostle of Jesus Christ, To those who through the righteousness of our God and Savior Jesus Christ have received a faith as precious as ours: ²Grace and peace be yours in abundance through the knowledge of God and of Jesus our Lord.

Making One's Calling and Election Sure

³His divine power has given us everything we need for life and godliness through our knowledge of him who called us by his own glory and goodness. ⁴Through these he has given us his very great and precious promises, so that through them you may participate in the divine nature and escape the corruption in the world caused by evil desires. ⁵For this very reason, make every effort to add to your faith goodness; and to goodness, knowledge; ⁶and to knowledge, self-control; and to self-control, perseverance; and to perseverance, godliness; ⁷and to godliness, brotherly kindness; and to brotherly kindness, love. ⁸For if you possess these qualities in increasing measure, they will keep you from being ineffective and unproductive in your knowledge of our Lord Jesus Christ.

There will be times that false teachers will approach you to confuse your position in God and your direction in life. Don't get confused by the ability of some people to sound intellectual and persuasive. Satan has some very impressive and seductive mouthpieces. In this season, you have to be careful about who prays over you as well as who you allow to speak into your life. You are what you eat spiritually.

Wash Me

Psalm 51:1-6 (New International Version)

¹ Have mercy on me, O God, according to your unfailing love; according to your great compassion blot out my transgressions. ² Wash away all my iniquity and cleanse me from my sin. ³ For I know my transgressions, and my sin is always before me. ⁴ Against you, you only, have I sinned and done what is evil in your sight, so that you are proved right when you speak and justified when you judge. ⁵ Surely I was sinful at birth, sinful from the time my mother conceived me. ⁶ Surely you desire truth in the inner parts you teach me wisdom in the inmost place.

Psalm 51 is one of my favorite passages in the bible. It demonstrates how to fix something in your life that has been broken. Each of us is confronted with the presence of sin in our lives daily. Sometimes that presence will lead to behavior that is damaging and destructive. Sin has the ability to make us feel dirty and unworthy. If you ever begin feeling this way, ask God to wash you. The presence of the spirit will wash away guilt, hurt, shame and anger. Get it right with God and watch God clean it up with everybody else. Start your day off by just saying, "Wash me Lord".

No Division

Ephesians 4:1-10 (New International Version)
Unity in the Body of Christ

¹As a prisoner for the Lord, then, I urge you to live a life worthy of the calling you have received. ²Be completely humble and gentle; be patient, bearing with one another in love. ³Make every effort to keep the unity of the Spirit through the bond of peace. ⁴There is one body and one Spirit—just as you were called to one hope when you were called— ⁵one Lord, one faith, one baptism; ⁶one God and Father of all, who is over all and through all and in all.

⁷But to each one of us grace has been given as Christ apportioned it. ⁸This is why it says: "When he ascended on high, he led captives in his train and gave gifts to men."⁹(What does "he ascended" mean except that he also descended to the lower, earthly regions? ¹⁰He who descended is the very one who ascended higher than all the heavens, in order to fill the whole universe.)

One of the oldest tricks in the book is to divide and conquer. Each day, Satan sets out to divide families and friends with the ultimate intent being to destroy by division. How many people are you no longer speaking to or are no longer speaking to you because of something small and petty? Don't allow the enemy space to creep in and create division.

When God Changes His Mind

Jonah 3:1-5 (New International Version)
Jonah Goes to Nineveh

¹ Then the word of the LORD came to Jonah a second time: ² "Go to the great city of Nineveh and proclaim to it the message I give you." ³ Jonah obeyed the word of the LORD and went to Nineveh. Now Nineveh was a very important city—a visit required three days. ⁴ On the first day, Jonah started into the city. He proclaimed: "Forty more days and Nineveh will be overturned." ⁵ The Ninevites believed God. They declared a fast, and all of them, from the greatest to the least, put on sackcloth.

I know there are those who subscribe to the theology that when God says something, He doesn't go back on what He said. Each day my feet hit the ground is a fresh reminder to me about how awesome the love and grace of God really is. There may be plenty of people you know that have their own opinion about you. There is nothing you can do to change that. Be thankful today because God is not like that. He leaves himself room to move around in our lives. Thank God for all the times you did something that you should not have and God walked toward you instead of away from you. Let God change His mind because it might be the change you need.

Rev. Dr. James E. Jones, Jr.

Freedom With Limitation

1 Corinthians 8:1-13 (New International Version)
Food Sacrificed to Idols

¹Now about food sacrificed to idols: We know that we all possess knowledge. Knowledge puffs up, but love builds up. ²The man who thinks he knows something does not yet know as he ought to know. ³But the man who loves God is known by God. ⁴So then, about eating food sacrificed to idols: We know that an idol is nothing at all in the world and that there is no God but one. ⁵For even if there are so-called gods, whether in heaven or on earth (as indeed there are many "gods" and many "lords"), ⁶yet for us there is but one God, the Father, from whom all things came and for whom we live; and there is but one Lord, Jesus Christ, through whom all things came and through whom we live. ⁷But not everyone knows this. Some people are still so accustomed to idols that when they eat such food they think of it as having been sacrificed to an idol, and since their conscience is weak, it is defiled. ⁸But food does not bring us near to God; we are no worse if we do not eat, and no better if we do. ⁹Be careful, however, that the exercise of your freedom does not become a stumbling block to the weak. ¹⁰For if anyone with a weak conscience sees you who have this knowledge eating in an idol's temple, won't he be emboldened to eat what has been sacrificed to idols? ¹¹So this weak brother, for whom Christ died, is destroyed by your knowledge. ¹²When you sin against your brothers in this way and wound their weak conscience, you sin against Christ. ¹³Therefore, if what I eat causes my brother to fall into sin, I will never eat meat again, so that I will not cause him to fall.

God is God of free will. God allows us the power and freedom to make our own decisions. You and I have the freedom to do and say whatever we feel. Expression is about freedom and our freedom comes as a result of God.

Some things may look and feel good to you but they may not be good for you. Don't waste another second or another day. Make the right choice. Acknowledge your limitations but excel because your expectation is bigger than your limitation.

God is Still In Charge

Psalm 52:7-10 (New International Version)

⁷ "Here now is the man who did not make God his stronghold but trusted in his great wealth and grew strong by destroying others!" ⁸ But I am like an olive tree flourishing in the house of God; I trust in God's unfailing love for ever and ever. ⁹ I will praise you forever for what you have done; in your name I will hope, for your name is good. I will praise you in the presence of your saints.

Throughout the word, many people have fallen on tough times. With the unemployment rate escalating, each day our hope seems to be evaporating. How do we find strength just to make it another day? No matter who is in power, God is always in charge. God is working on the outcome of your situation even now. No matter who it is or what it is, God has the last word over your situation. Rest easy, God is in charge.

Rev. Dr. James E. Jones, Jr.

Where Is My Healing

Jeremiah 8:18-22 (New International Version)

[18] O my Comforter in sorrow, my heart is faint within me. [19] Listen to the cry of my people from a land far away: "Is the LORD not in Zion? Is her King no longer there?" "Why have they provoked me to anger with their images, with their worthless foreign idols?" [20] "The harvest is past, the summer has ended, and we are not saved." [21] Since my people are crushed, I am crushed; I mourn, and horror grips me. [22] Is there no balm in Gilead? Is there no physician there? Why then is there no healing for the wound of my people?

Many of us have tried so many different things to ease our pain. We have tried alcohol, drugs, sex and many other painful social ills. Nothing seems to satisfy the deep longing in your soul or the pain in your heart. Day after day you walk around as if you've got it all together when in all actuality, you are falling apart at the seams. The best healing for a wounded soul is Jesus. Let Him touch you right where the pain is.

Just Keep Believing

Psalm 31:9-16 (New International Version)

⁹ Be merciful to me, O LORD, for I am in distress; my eyes grow weak with sorrow, my soul and my body with grief. ¹⁰ My life is consumed by anguish and my years by groaning; my strength fails because of my affliction, and my bones grow weak. ¹¹ Because of all my enemies, I am the utter contempt of my neighbors; I am a dread to my friends— those who see me on the street flee from me.

¹² I am forgotten by them as though I were dead; I have become like broken pottery. ¹³ For I hear the slander of many; there is terror on every side; they conspire against me and plot to take my life. ¹⁴ But I trust in you, O LORD; I say, "You are my God." ¹⁵ My times are in your hands; deliver me from my enemies and from those who pursue me. ¹⁶ Let your face shine on your servant; save me in your unfailing love.

Life has a way of making us question what we believe or who we believe in. There are times when life can become so tough, that it even makes us question ourselves. Today, God wants to encourage your heart that you are headed in the right direction. It may not seem like it or look like it right now but the road you are on is exactly the road God wants you to be on in this season. Don't turn around or shift to the right or left, your breakthrough is at the end of the road.

It Won't Break Me

1 Kings 19:1-15 (New International Version)
Elijah Flees to Horeb

¹ Now Ahab told Jezebel everything Elijah had done and how he had killed all the prophets with the sword. ² So Jezebel sent a messenger to Elijah to say, "May the gods deal with me, be it ever so severely, if by this time tomorrow I do not make your life like that of one of them." ³ Elijah was afraid and ran for his life. When he came to Beersheba in Judah, he left his servant there, ⁴ while he himself went a day's journey into the desert. He came to a broom tree, sat down under it and prayed that he might die. "I have had enough, LORD," he said. "Take my life; I am no better than my ancestors." ⁵ Then he lay down under the tree and fell asleep. All at once an angel touched him and said, "Get up and eat." ⁶ He looked around, and there by his head was a cake of bread baked over hot coals, and a jar of water. He ate and drank and then lay down again. ⁷ The angel of the LORD came back a second time and touched him and said, "Get up and eat, for the journey is too much for you." ⁸ So he got up and ate and drank. Strengthened by that food, he traveled forty days and forty nights until he reached Horeb, the mountain of God. ⁹There he went into a cave and spent the night.

The LORD Appears to Elijah

And the word of the LORD came to him: "What are you doing here, Elijah?" ¹⁰ He replied, "I have been very zealous for the LORD God Almighty. The Israelites have rejected your covenant, broken down your altars, and put your prophets to death with the sword. I am the only one left, and now they are trying to kill me too." ¹¹ The LORD said, "Go out and stand on the mountain in the presence of the LORD, for the LORD is about to pass by." Then a great and powerful wind tore the mountains apart and shattered the rocks before the LORD, but the LORD was not in the wind. After the wind there was an earthquake, but the LORD was not in the earthquake. ¹² After the earthquake came a fire, but the LORD was not in the fire. And after the fire came a gentle whisper. ¹³ When Elijah heard it, he pulled his cloak over his face and went out and stood at the mouth of the cave. Then a voice said to him, "What are you doing here, Elijah?" ¹⁴ He replied, "I have been very zealous for the LORD God Almighty. The Israelites have rejected your covenant, broken down your altars, and put

your prophets to death with the sword. I am the only one left, and now they are trying to kill me too."
¹⁵ The LORD said to him, "Go back the way you came, and go to the Desert of Damascus. When you get there, anoint Hazael king over Aram.

Sometimes in life we feel as though we are at our breaking point. The breaking point is that stressful place in life where you feel like you just can't handle one more piece of bad news. The breaking point is that place where you have cried so much, you are out of tears. The breaking point is when you have become so frustrated that you have reached a boiling point. You feel as if the wrong thing happens, you could lose control.

The next time you find yourself dealing with one of life's breaking moments, remember these 3 things:
1. Realize God is still speaking to you
2. Realize God is about to move
3. Realize God has blessings on reserve

Expect the Unexpected

Revelation 21:1-5 (New International Version)
The New Jerusalem

¹Then I saw a new heaven and a new earth, for the first heaven and the first earth had passed away, and there was no longer any sea. ²I saw the Holy City, the new Jerusalem, coming down out of heaven from God, prepared as a bride beautifully dressed for her husband. ³And I heard a loud voice from the throne saying, "Now the dwelling of God is with men, and he will live with them. They will be his people, and God himself will be with them and be their God. ⁴He will wipe every tear from their eyes. There will be no more death or mourning or crying or pain, for the old order of things has passed away." ⁵He who was seated on the throne said, "I am making everything new!" Then he said, "Write this down, for these words are trustworthy and true."

For many people, life has become like one giant merry-go-round. In other words, life sometimes makes a lot of movement but very little progress. Many people live life feeling trapped or stuck. It is as if each day begins and ends the exact same way. Today, God desires to bless you in an unexpected manner.

The question of the day is: How do you receive unexpected blessings? Believe that based upon what He has already done, things are about to change. Develop the spirit of a conqueror and not a coward. In life, sometimes we have to cheer ourselves on. If nobody can see it or believe it, you should get excited today about your own future.

God is ready to do the unexpected in your life, are you?

Say Something

Job 40:1-10 (New International Version)
¹ The LORD said to Job: ² "Will the one who contends with the Almighty correct him? Let him who accuses God answer him!" ³ Then Job answered the LORD : ⁴ "I am unworthy—how can I reply to you? I put my hand over my mouth. ⁵ I spoke once, but I have no answer— twice, but I will say no more." ⁶ Then the LORD spoke to Job out of the storm: ⁷ "Brace yourself like a man; I will question you, and you shall answer me. ⁸ "Would you discredit my justice? Would you condemn me to justify yourself? ⁹ Do you have an arm like God's, and can your voice thunder like his? ¹⁰ Then adorn yourself with glory and splendor, and clothe yourself in honor and majesty.

Recently, I came across a song from one of the more popular rap artists, Timberland. The title of the song was "Say Something". My attention was immediately arrested as I listened. Then I raised the question to myself: How many times have I walked around silent because I didn't understand what God was doing in my life?

Have you ever just had one of those seasons in which things didn't add up or the pieces of life didn't fit? In those moments, God just wants you to say something.

Remember this: God can handle your questions. Your questions are not about His authority but His actions. Say it to God. Just keep in mind that God reserves the exclusive right to say anything back to you.

Working Together

1 Corinthians 12 (New International Version)
Spiritual Gifts

¹Now about spiritual gifts, brothers, I do not want you to be ignorant. ²You know that when you were pagans, somehow or other you were influenced and led astray to mute idols. ³Therefore I tell you that no one who is speaking by the Spirit of God says, "Jesus be cursed," and no one can say, "Jesus is Lord," except by the Holy Spirit. ⁴There are different kinds of gifts, but the same Spirit. ⁵There are different kinds of service, but the same Lord. ⁶There are different kinds of working, but the same God works all of them in all men. ⁷Now to each one the manifestation of the Spirit is given for the common good. ⁸To one there is given through the Spirit the message of wisdom, to another the message of knowledge by means of the same Spirit, ⁹to another faith by the same Spirit, to another gifts of healing by that one Spirit, ¹⁰to another miraculous powers, to another prophecy, to another distinguishing between spirits, to another speaking in different kinds of tongues, and to still another the interpretation of tongues. ¹¹All these are the work of one and the same Spirit, and he gives them to each one, just as he determines. ¹²The body is a unit, though it is made up of many parts; and though all its parts are many, they form one body. So it is with Christ. ¹³For we were all baptized by one Spirit into one body—whether Jews or Greeks, slave or free—and we were all given the one Spirit to drink. ¹⁴Now the body is not made up of one part but of many. ¹⁵If the foot should say, "Because I am not a hand, I do not belong to the body," it would not for that reason cease to be part of the body. ¹⁶And if the ear should say, "Because I am not an eye, I do not belong to the body," it would not for that reason cease to be part of the body. ¹⁷If the whole body were an eye, where would the sense of hearing be? If the whole body were an ear, where would the sense of smell be? ¹⁸But in fact God has arranged the parts in the body, every one of them, just as he wanted them to be. ¹⁹If they were all one part, where would the body be? ²⁰As it is, there are many parts, but one body. ²¹The eye cannot say to the hand, "I don't need you!" And the head cannot say to the feet, "I don't need you!" ²²On the contrary, those parts of the body that seem to be weaker are indispensable, ²³and the parts that we think are less honorable we treat with special honor. And the parts that are unpresentable are treated with special modesty, ²⁴while our presentable parts need no special treatment. But God has combined the members of the body and has given greater honor to the parts that lacked it, ²⁵*so that there should be no division in the body, but that its parts should have equal concern for each other.* ²⁶*If one part suffers, every part suffers with it; if one part is honored, every part rejoices with it.* ²⁷*Now you are the body of Christ, and each one of you is a part of it.* ²⁸*And in the church God has appointed first of all apostles, second prophets, third teachers, then workers of miracles, also those having gifts of healing, those able to help others, those with gifts of administration, and those speaking in different kinds of tongues.* ²⁹*Are all apostles? Are all prophets? Are all teachers? Do all work miracles?* ³⁰*Do all have gifts of healing? Do all speak in tongues? Do all interpret?* ³¹*But eagerly desire the greater gifts. And now I will show you the most excellent way.*

Life can get the best of us, if we are not careful. Most of us lean more to our strengths and try to avoid those areas of weakness. If you ever want to turn some of your weaknesses into strengths, start focusing more energy in those areas. When you are spiritually, emotionally, physically and financially strong, positive things are bound to happen. Three things happen when everything is working together:

1. You will have power
2. You will experience peace
3. You will live in prosperity

Rev. Dr. James E. Jones, Jr.

It Hurts But Keep Going

Romans 11:1-11 (New International Version)
The Remnant of Israel

¹I ask then: Did God reject his people? By no means! I am an Israelite myself, a descendant of Abraham, from the tribe of Benjamin. ²God did not reject his people, whom he foreknew. Don't you know what the Scripture says in the passage about Elijah—how he appealed to God against Israel: ³"Lord, they have killed your prophets and torn down your altars; I am the only one left, and they are trying to kill me"? ⁴And what was God's answer to him? "I have reserved for myself seven thousand who have not bowed the knee to Baal." ⁵So too, at the present time there is a remnant chosen by grace. ⁶And if by grace, then it is no longer by works; if it were, grace would no longer be grace. ⁷What then? What Israel sought so earnestly it did not obtain, but the elect did. The others were hardened, ⁸as it is written: "God gave them a spirit of stupor, eyes so that they could not see and ears so that they could not hear, to this very day." ⁹And David says: "May their table become a snare and a trap, a stumbling block and a retribution for them. ¹⁰May their eyes be darkened so they cannot see, and their backs be bent forever."

Ingrafted Branches

¹¹Again I ask: Did they stumble so as to fall beyond recovery? Not at all! Rather, because of their transgression, salvation has come to the Gentiles to make Israel envious.

Today might be one of those days that the emotional or physical pain just seems to get you down and you have no energy to keep pushing. Life is like that sometimes. Whether it is emotional pain that seems to keep you confined to the bed or physical pain that limits any type of movement, both can be debilitating.

I remember catching a cramp in my side while exercising. For the life of me, I thought I would feel better if I sat down. To my surprise, my trainer told me that sitting down would make it worse. He instructed me that the best treatment for the pain was to keep walking until I walked it out. Our personal pain should be addressed the same way.

It is easy to stop when things get hard but your spiritual muscles develop endurance when you don't give up. Don't give up or give in. Keep going!

It Really Doesn't Matter

Luke 12:22-31 (New International Version)
Do Not Worry

²²Then Jesus said to his disciples: "Therefore I tell you, do not worry about your life, what you will eat; or about your body, what you will wear. ²³Life is more than food, and the body more than clothes. ²⁴Consider the ravens: They do not sow or reap, they have no storeroom or barn; yet God feeds them. And how much more valuable you are than birds! ²⁵Who of you by worrying can add a single hour to his life? ²⁶Since you cannot do this very little thing, why do you worry about the rest? ²⁷"Consider how the lilies grow. They do not labor or spin. Yet I tell you, not even Solomon in all his splendor was dressed like one of these. ²⁸If that is how God clothes the grass of the field, which is here today, and tomorrow is thrown into the fire, how much more will he clothe you, O you of little faith! ²⁹And do not set your heart on what you will eat or drink; do not worry about it. ³⁰For the pagan world runs after all such things, and your Father knows that you need them. ³¹But seek his kingdom, and these things will be given to you as well.

How many people do you know who are constantly worried about tomorrow when tomorrow hasn't even arrived yet? We worry about so many different things from where we are going to live to the kind of car we drive. We worry about food, clothes and paying bills. I am not sure of the last time you were worried about something or someone but the next time it happens, reflect on the following:

Learn how to live in the moment. Yesterday is dead and tomorrow has not yet been born. The key is to do the best you can with your right now. See your situation as small stuff to a big God. God is not sweating it so why are you? Suggesting that something does not matter is not a sign that someone does not care but a sign that somebody knows who is in control.

The Blessing of Succession

Luke 1:46-55 (New International Version)
Mary's Song

[46] *And Mary said: "My soul glorifies the Lord* [47] *and my spirit rejoices in God my Savior,* [48] *for he has been mindful of the humble state of his servant. From now on all generations will call me blessed,* [49] *for the Mighty One has done great things for me— holy is his name.* [50] *His mercy extends to those who fear him, from generation to generation.* [51] *He has performed mighty deeds with his arm; he has scattered those who are proud in their inmost thoughts.* [52] *He has brought down rulers from their thrones but has lifted up the humble.* [53] *He has filled the hungry with good things but has sent the rich away empty.* [54] *He has helped his servant Israel, remembering to be merciful* [55] *to Abraham and his descendants forever, even as he said to our fathers."*

God desires for all of his children to be blessed. You should not only look blessed but live blessed. The problem with some of our blessings is that they stop with us. God's blessings should not just flow in you but through you. My father once told me, "Son, I want you to be better than me." Even though my father was blessed, it was his desire that my blessing flow further than his

We must not get caught up in just living for today but we must pass a blessing down. Don't let your blessings stop with you. You should desire to be so blessed that your blessings are seen from one generation to the next. You're not blessed to show off, you're blessed to pass a blessing down.

Dedicated and Disciplined

Jeremiah 27:1-13 (New International Version)
Judah to Serve Nebuchadnezzar

¹ Early in the reign of Zedekiah son of Josiah king of Judah, this word came to Jeremiah from the LORD : ² This is what the LORD said to me: "Make a yoke out of straps and crossbars and put it on your neck. ³ Then send word to the kings of Edom, Moab, Ammon, Tyre and Sidon through the envoys who have come to Jerusalem to Zedekiah king of Judah. ⁴ Give them a message for their masters and say, 'This is what the LORD Almighty, the God of Israel, says: "Tell this to your masters: ⁵ With my great power and outstretched arm I made the earth and its people and the animals that are on it, and I give it to anyone I please. ⁶ Now I will hand all your countries over to my servant Nebuchadnezzar king of Babylon; I will make even the wild animals subject to him. ⁷ All nations will serve him and his son and his grandson until the time for his land comes; then many nations and great kings will subjugate him. ⁸ " ' "If, however, any nation or kingdom will not serve Nebuchadnezzar king of Babylon or bow its neck under his yoke, I will punish that nation with the sword, famine and plague, declares the LORD, until I destroy it by his hand. ⁹ So do not listen to your prophets, your diviners, your interpreters of dreams, your mediums or your sorcerers who tell you, 'You will not serve the king of Babylon.' ¹⁰ They prophesy lies to you that will only serve to remove you far from your lands; I will banish you and you will perish. ¹¹ But if any nation will bow its neck under the yoke of the king of Babylon and serve him, I will let that nation remain in its own land to till it and to live there, declares the LORD." ' " ¹² I gave the same message to Zedekiah king of Judah. I said, "Bow your neck under the yoke of the king of Babylon; serve him and his people, and you will live. ¹³ Why will you and your people die by the sword, famine and plague with which the LORD has threatened any nation that will not serve the king of Babylon?

Show me someone who is lazy and I will show you someone who won't get very far in life. On the flip side, show me someone who works hard every day and I will show you someone who will eventually experience success. Discipline is necessary in order for you to successfully follow God. The ability to do something positive over and over again will produce positive results. Repetition without relationship is dangerous. Repetition with relationship produces power.

Pray every day, work hard, play hard and most definitely pray hard. Go hard for God!

❧ ❧ ❧ ❧ ❧ ❧ ❧ ❧ ❧ ❧ ❧ ❧ ❧ ❧ ❧

When Nobody Seems To Care

Micah 7:1-7 (New International Version)
Israel's Misery

¹ What misery is mine! I am like one who gathers summer fruit at the gleaning of the vineyard; there is no cluster of grapes to eat, none of the early figs that I crave.
² The godly have been swept from the land; not one upright man remains. All men lie in wait to shed blood; each hunts his brother with a net. ³ Both hands are skilled in doing evil; the ruler demands gifts, the judge accepts bribes, the powerful dictate what they desire— they all conspire together. ⁴ The best of them is like a brier, the most upright worse than a thorn hedge. The day of your watchmen has come, the day God visits you. Now is the time of their confusion. ⁵ Do not trust a neighbor; put no confidence in a friend. Even with her who lies in your embrace be careful of your words. ⁶ For a son dishonors his father, a daughter rises up against her mother, a daughter-in-law against her mother-in-law — a man's enemies are the members of his own household. ⁷ But as for me, I watch in hope for the LORD, I wait for God my Savior; my God will hear me.

There are times in life when it seems as though the things you want the most are the hardest to achieve. In addition, it seems no one cares that you can't achieve them. Sometimes the only difference between a good day and a bad day is someone who will listen. You may feel as if you are there for everyone else but no one is around for you when you need a friend.

In those tough moments, be encouraged. Know that God cares when nobody else does. He loves you and is concerned about your progress.

Where Were You?

Job 38:4-10 (New International Version)
⁴ "Where were you when I laid the earth's foundation? Tell me, if you understand. ⁵ Who marked off its dimensions? Surely you know! Who stretched a measuring line across it? ⁶ On what were its footings set, or who laid its cornerstone- ⁷ while the morning stars sang together and all the angels shouted for joy? ⁸ "Who shut up the sea behind doors when it burst forth from the womb, ⁹ when I made the clouds its garment and wrapped it in thick darkness, ¹⁰ when I fixed limits for it and set its doors and bars in place,

Recently, I have encountered a great amount of sickness and death. So much that it causes me to want to question God. "Why?" seems like such a relevant question to ask God in times like these. Why am I going through this? Why do my kids treat me like this? Why can't I find a job? Why am I alone? Questioning God makes so much sense.

However, if I were you, before I question God again I would think twice. Why? Because you may not be ready for his response.

Trust the Promise

2 Kings 5:1-14 (New International Version)
Naaman Healed of Leprosy
¹ Now Naaman was commander of the army of the king of Aram. He was a great man in the sight of his master and highly regarded, because through him the LORD had given victory to Aram. He was a valiant soldier, but he had leprosy. ² Now bands from Aram had gone out and had taken captive a young girl from Israel, and she served Naaman's wife. ³ She said to her mistress, "If only my master would see the prophet who is in Samaria! He would cure him of his leprosy." ⁴ Naaman went to his master and told him what the girl from Israel had said. ⁵ "By all means, go," the king of Aram replied. "I will send a letter to the king of Israel." So Naaman left, taking with him ten talents of silver, six thousand shekels of gold and ten sets of

clothing. ⁶ The letter that he took to the king of Israel read: "With this letter I am sending my servant Naaman to you so that you may cure him of his leprosy." ⁷ As soon as the king of Israel read the letter, he tore his robes and said, "Am I God? Can I kill and bring back to life? Why does this fellow send someone to me to be cured of his leprosy? See how he is trying to pick a quarrel with me!" ⁸ When Elisha the man of God heard that the king of Israel had torn his robes, he sent him this message: "Why have you torn your robes? Have the man come to me and he will know that there is a prophet in Israel." ⁹ So Naaman went with his horses and chariots and stopped at the door of Elisha's house. ¹⁰ Elisha sent a messenger to say to him, "Go, wash yourself seven times in the Jordan, and your flesh will be restored and you will be cleansed." ¹¹ But Naaman went away angry and said, "I thought that he would surely come out to me and stand and call on the name of the LORD his God, wave his hand over the spot and cure me of my leprosy. ¹² Are not Abana and Pharpar, the rivers of Damascus, better than any of the waters of Israel? Couldn't I wash in them and be cleansed?" So he turned and went off in a rage. ¹³ Naaman's servants went to him and said, "My father, if the prophet had told you to do some great thing, would you not have done it? How much more, then, when he tells you, 'Wash and be cleansed'!" ¹⁴ So he went down and dipped himself in the Jordan seven times, as the man of God had told him, and his flesh was restored and became clean like that of a young boy.

Since I can remember, I have believed promises were made to be kept but easily broken. Every day, someone is breaking a promise to a family member, a friend or a co-worker. I have discovered that God is the ultimate promise keeper. God is multidimensional. He can be everywhere and do everything at the same time. When everything has failed you, hold on to the promise. It will keep you when everything else has failed you. God would not have said it if He was not able to perform it. Trust the promise, not your sight.

Get A Piece of the Rock

Psalm 62 (New International Version)

[1] My soul finds rest in God alone; my salvation comes from him. [2] He alone is my rock and my salvation; he is my fortress, I will never be shaken. [3] How long will you assault a man? Would all of you throw him down— this leaning wall, this tottering fence? [4] They fully intend to topple him from his lofty place; they take delight in lies. With their mouths they bless, but in their hearts they curse. Selah [5] Find rest, O my soul, in God alone; my hope comes from him. [6] He alone is my rock and my salvation; he is my fortress, I will not be shaken. [7] My salvation and my honor depend on God [a] ; he is my mighty rock, my refuge.[8] Trust in him at all times, O people; pour out your hearts to him, for God is our refuge. Selah [9] Lowborn men are but a breath, the highborn are but a lie; if weighed on a balance, they are nothing; together they are only a breath. [10] Do not trust in extortion or take pride in stolen goods; though your riches increase, do not set your heart on them. [11] One thing God has spoken, two things have I heard: that you, O God, are strong, [12] and that you, O Lord, are loving. Surely you will reward each person according to what he has done.

When you see the slogan "Get A Piece of the Rock", insurance usually comes to mind. Biblically, this phrase means much more. In times of instability, you can find strength in God because God is unmovable, unshakeable and unbreakable. Insurance is important and the best policy you can have is lifetime assurance.

If you died at this moment, where would you spend eternity? Keep God in your life and no matter how unstable times get, you will not be shaken.

God Is With You

Judges 6:11-16 (New International Version)

¹¹ The angel of the LORD came and sat down under the oak in Ophrah that belonged to Joash the Abiezrite, where his son Gideon was threshing wheat in a winepress to keep it from the Midianites. ¹² When the angel of the LORD appeared to Gideon, he said, "The LORD is with you, mighty warrior." ¹³ "But sir," Gideon replied, "if the LORD is with us, why has all this happened to us? Where are all his wonders that our fathers told us about when they said, 'Did not the LORD bring us up out of Egypt?' But now the LORD has abandoned us and put us into the hand of Midian." ¹⁴ The LORD turned to him and said, "Go in the strength you have and save Israel out of Midian's hand. Am I not sending you?" ¹⁵ "But Lord", Gideon asked, "how can I save Israel? My clan is the weakest in Manasseh, and I am the least in my family." ¹⁶ The LORD answered, "I will be with you, and you will strike down all the Midianites together."

Have you ever felt alone or abandoned? Jesus did when He hung on the cross and asked God why. Many of us have had moments where we wrestled with the presence of God versus the absence of God. Today, God wants you to be encouraged and reminded that he is with you. There is not an hour or a moment that God is not with us. You may be facing some tough challenges today but don't be afraid or nervous. God is with you every step of the way. You are not alone.

Take Care of Your Temple

1 Corinthians 6:12-20 (New International Version)

¹²"Everything is permissible for me"—but not everything is beneficial. "Everything is permissible for me"—but I will not be mastered by anything. ¹³"Food for the stomach and the stomach for food"—but God will destroy them both. The body is not meant for sexual immorality, but for the Lord, and the Lord for the body. ¹⁴By his power God raised the Lord from the dead, and he will raise us also. ¹⁵Do you not know that your bodies are members of Christ himself? Shall I then take the members of Christ and unite them with a prostitute? Never! ¹⁶Do you not know that he who unites himself with a prostitute is one with her in body? For it is said, "The two will become one flesh." ¹⁷But he who unites himself with the Lord is one with him in spirit. ¹⁸Flee from sexual immorality. All other sins a man commits are outside his body, but he who sins sexually sins against his own body. ¹⁹Do you not know that your body is a temple of the Holy Spirit, who is in you, whom you have received from God? You are not your own; ²⁰you were bought at a price. Therefore honor God with your body.

My mother used to always say that no matter how good iron is, it will eventually wear out. Our bodies are our personal temples. We only get one body and it is our responsibility to take care of it. It is important that we eat right, get plenty of rest and exercise daily. We only get one temple and it is vital to take care of it. Don't abuse God's investment.

Rev. Dr. James E. Jones, Jr.

New Direction

Luke 19:1-10 (New International Version)
Zacchaeus the Tax Collector

¹Jesus entered Jericho and was passing through. ²A man was there by the name of Zacchaeus; he was a chief tax collector and was wealthy. ³He wanted to see who Jesus was, but being a short man he could not, because of the crowd. ⁴So he ran ahead and climbed a sycamore-fig tree to see him, since Jesus was coming that way. ⁵When Jesus reached the spot, he looked up and said to him, "Zacchaeus, come down immediately. I must stay at your house today." ⁶So he came down at once and welcomed him gladly. ⁷All the people saw this and began to mutter, "He has gone to be the guest of a 'sinner.' " ⁸But Zacchaeus stood up and said to the Lord, "Look, Lord! Here and now I give half of my possessions to the poor, and if I have cheated anybody out of anything, I will pay back four times the amount." ⁹Jesus said to him, "Today salvation has come to this house, because this man, too, is a son of Abraham. ¹⁰For the Son of Man came to seek and to save what was lost."

As you take a look at our world, most everything we do operates on time. We experience new days, new months, new weeks, new years and new opportunities. There are moments in our lives that God desires to take us into a new direction. This may represent for you a season where God is calling you to do something new. The friends you have, the places you go, the habits you have developed and the emptiness sometimes experienced all may need a change of direction. If you have been traveling north, head south. If you have been going east, change direction and go west. Go a different way today if you want to experience something different.

Wisdom Over Wealth

Psalm 111 (New International Version)
¹ Praise the LORD. I will extol the LORD with all my *heart in the council of the upright and in the assembly.* ²*Great are the works of the LORD; they are pondered by all who delight in them.* ³ *Glorious and majestic are his deeds, and his righteousness endures forever.* ⁴ *He has caused his wonders to be remembered; the LORD is gracious and compassionate.* ⁵ *He provides food for those who fear him; he remembers his covenant forever.* ⁶ *He has shown his people the power of his works, giving them the lands of other nations.* ⁷ *The works of his hands are faithful and just; all his precepts are trustworthy.* ⁸ *They are steadfast for ever and ever, done in faithfulness and uprightness.* ⁹ *He provided redemption for his people; he ordained his covenant forever— holy and awesome is his name.* ¹⁰ *The fear of the LORD is the beginning of wisdom; all who follow his precepts have good understanding. To him belongs eternal praise.*

In our fast paced society, we see fast cars, fast food and many of us are chasing fast money. Our world is filled with people chasing wealth. This is dangerous if wisdom does not travel with wealth. If you are not wise with your possessions, you will lose them. There is nothing wrong with being wealthy or having a desire to be wealthy, just desire to be wise before becoming wealthy so that you don't blow your fortune.

Rev. Dr. James E. Jones, Jr.

Worship the Lord

Psalm 103 (New International Version)

¹Praise the LORD, O my soul; all my inmost being, praise his holy name. ² Praise the LORD, O my soul, and forget not all his benefits- ³ who forgives all your sins and heals all your diseases, ⁴ who redeems your life from the pit and crowns you with love and compassion, ⁵ who satisfies your desires with good things so that your youth is renewed like the eagle's. ⁶ The LORD works righteousness and justice for all the oppressed. ⁷ He made known his ways to Moses, his deeds to the people of Israel: ⁸ The LORD is compassionate and gracious, slow to anger, abounding in love. ⁹ He will not always accuse, nor will he harbor his anger forever; ¹⁰ he does not treat us as our sins deserve or repay us according to our iniquities. ¹¹ For as high as the heavens are above the earth, so great is his love for those who fear him; ¹² as far as the east is from the west, so far has he removed our transgressions from us. ¹³ As a father has compassion on his children, so the LORD has compassion on those who fear him; ¹⁴ for he knows how we are formed, he remembers that we are dust. ¹⁵ As for man, his days are like grass, he flourishes like a flower of the field; ¹⁶ the wind blows over it and it is gone, and its place remembers it no more. ¹⁷ But from everlasting to everlasting the LORD's love is with those who fear him, and his righteousness with their children's children- ¹⁸ with those who keep his covenant and remember to obey his precepts. ¹⁹ The LORD has established his throne in heaven, and his kingdom rules over all. ²⁰ Praise the LORD, you his angels, you mighty ones who do his bidding, who obey his word. ²¹ Praise the LORD, all his heavenly hosts, you his servants who do his will. ²² Praise the LORD, all his works everywhere in his dominion. Praise the LORD, O my soul.

There is nothing that can compare to worshipping God. Worship heals you. Worship touches you. Worship releases you. Worship breaks you. Worship humbles you.

Maybe that is why your day is going the way it is, simply because you did not worship Him today. Every day is a day of thanksgiving. He is God and He is everything. We praise Him for what He has done and we worship Him for who He is.

Time is Drawing Near

1 Corinthians 7:29-31 (New International Version)
[29]What I mean, brothers, is that the time is short. From now on those who have wives should live as if they had none; [30]those who mourn, as if they did not; those who are happy, as if they were not; those who buy something, as if it were not theirs to keep; [31]those who use the things of the world, as if not engrossed in them. For this world in its present form is passing away.

The other day, I was having a conversation with an associate. The gentleman shared with me how he wasn't scared of anything, including death. Be careful of inflating the idea that nothing can break you. God has a situation that can break all of us. Time is swiftly moving. This is not time to be bitter or hold grudges because you never know what tomorrow might bring. Make peace with yourself, your neighbor but more importantly with God.

God Gave It To You

1 Chronicles 29:11-13 (New International Version)
¹¹ Yours, O LORD, is the greatness and the power and the glory and the majesty and the splendor, for everything in heaven and earth is yours. Yours, O LORD, is the kingdom; you are exalted as head over all. ¹² Wealth and honor come from you; you are the ruler of all things. In your hands are strength and power to exalt and give strength to all. ¹³ Now, our God, we give you thanks, and praise your glorious name.

God has been so good to you and its not because you have earned or deserve it. God gives to us simply because God's nature is to give. Sometimes we forget or we develop acute amnesia about who gave us the ability to breathe. It was God. Always remember that everything you have belongs to God. You don't own it. Though you may have the title, it belongs to God. If you don't believe it, die and see if you can take those things you own with you.

Thank God today, for every good and perfect gift comes from above.

❦❦❦❦❦❦❦❦❦❦❦❦❦❦❦❦❦

I've Been Changed

Psalm 145 (New International Version)
¹ I will exalt you, my God the King; I will praise your name for ever and ever. ² Every day I will praise you and extol your name for ever and ever. ³ Great is the LORD and most worthy of praise; his greatness no one can fathom. ⁴ One generation will commend your works to another; they will tell of your mighty acts. ⁵ They will speak of the glorious splendor of your majesty, and I will meditate on your wonderful works. ⁶ They will tell of the power of your awesome works, and I will proclaim your great deeds. ⁷ They will celebrate your abundant goodness and joyfully sing of your righteousness. ⁸ The LORD is gracious and compassionate, slow to anger and rich in love. ⁹ The LORD is good to all; he has compassion on all he has made. ¹⁰ All you have made will praise you, O LORD; your saints will extol you. ¹¹ They will tell of the glory of your kingdom and speak of your might, ¹² so that all men

may know of your mighty acts and the glorious splendor of your kingdom.
¹³ Your kingdom is an everlasting kingdom, and your dominion endures
through all generations. The LORD is faithful to all his promises and loving
toward all he has made. ¹⁴ The LORD upholds all those who fall and lifts up
all who are bowed down. ¹⁵ The eyes of all look to you, and you give them
their food at the proper time. ¹⁶ You open your hand and satisfy the desires
of every living thing. ¹⁷ The LORD is righteous in all his ways and loving
toward all he has made. ¹⁸ The LORD is near to all who call on him, to all
who call on him in truth. ¹⁹ He fulfills the desires of those who fear him;
he hears their cry and saves them. ²⁰ The LORD watches over all who love
him, but all the wicked he will destroy. ²¹ My mouth will speak in praise of
the LORD. Let every creature praise his holy name for ever and ever.

Change is not easy but is effective. Sometimes we put so much energy in
trying to keep things the way they are. Many of us fear change because
we have gotten comfortable with our current system of control. However,
I want to argue that change is not a bad thing but actually something
we should welcome and look forward to. I am sure much around you
has already changed. However, the object of your celebration today is
"celebrating the change within you." Don't ever apologize for changing,
it has actually made you a better person.

The Most Important Part

Proverbs 8:23-30 (New International Version)

²³ I was appointed from eternity, from the beginning, before the world began. ²⁴ When there were no oceans, I was given birth, when there were no springs abounding with water; ²⁵ before the mountains were settled in place, before the hills, I was given birth, ²⁶ before he made the earth or its fields or any of the dust of the world. ²⁷ I was there when he set the heavens in place, when he marked out the horizon on the face of the deep, ²⁸ when he established the clouds above and fixed securely the fountains of the deep, ²⁹ when he gave the sea its boundary so the waters would not overstep his command, and when he marked out the foundations of the earth. ³⁰ Then I was the craftsman at his side. I was filled with delight day after day, rejoicing always in his presence,

The most precious thing that any of us possess is not our money, houses or automobiles but our hearts. Your enemies would love nothing more than to tear your heart out and crush your spirit. The engine is one of the most important components of the car likewise your heart is a central component to who you are. Some people are trying to get close to you, so they can discover how to break you. In this season of your life, you must be careful who you give the access keys to your heart. God has so much invested in you, take time out today for protection over your heart,

When demonic intruders are getting too close to your heart, your spiritual radars must alert you that they have gotten too close. The only people in this season with access to your heart are those individuals who have your heart.

Shake It Off

Isaiah 55:1-2 (New International Version)
Invitation to the Thirsty

¹ "Come, all you who are thirsty, come to the waters; and you who have no money, come, buy and eat! Come, buy wine and milk without money and without cost. ² Why spend money on what is not bread, and your labor on what does not satisfy? Listen, listen to me, and eat what is good, and your soul will delight in the richest of fare.

Today is the day to SHAKE IT OFF! A story is told about a man who had a horse and because the horse didn't do everything the man thought he should, he decided to bury the horse. He dug a hole, placed the horse in it and began to shovel dirt on him. Some time passed and when the man looked up, the horse had gotten out of the hole. In disbelief, the man wondered how the horse got out. Every time the man threw dirt on the horse, the horse learned how to "shake it off" and "step up".

The next time somebody tries to throw dirt on you, "shake it off" and "step up".

Rev. Dr. James E. Jones, Jr.

The Power of Pentecost

The New Testament Church is birthed at Pentecost. This new birth or new beginning took place at Calvary nearly 50 days prior. That should be something to celebrate. Even now God is blessing us with something new.

Maybe you have a new job, new opportunity, new home, new car, new relationship, new attitude or new outlook. Whatever it is, you and I should be thankful for our new beginnings. This new beginning known as Pentecost allowed those who had run away in fear to now return. From the cross to the upper room, Pentecost has finally arrived.

The fifty day wait was finally over. Pentecost, which symbolizes the presence of God resting upon the people of God, had finally come. I believe this text also reminds us that sometimes some of our best blessings from God will take time to happen. We live in a world where you can have it your way right away. But my grandmother, who was never fortunate enough to graduate from a theological school or seminary, described it best by saying, "He may not come when you want Him to but He's always on time." God's timing on this day was perfect.

In verse 12, the text raises this very powerful question after the uproar that Pentecost has caused: What does all of this mean? In other words, what is the power of Pentecost?

Pentecost is about <u>position</u>. Sometimes we miss a blessing because we are in the wrong place but sometimes we can receive a blessing just for being in the right place. They were all gathered together in one place. The thing that fascinates me about this text is that they were not in the upper room or in the sanctuary. They were outside but God was with them.

Pentecost is about <u>power</u>. In verse 2, the text says *suddenly*. In other words, when God gets ready to move in your life. Sometimes God will move now.

God is not like a turtle. He can move quickly and precisely. He is also not like the 18 wheeler traveling down the highway. If it turns too quickly, it may turn over. God can turn the world, our situation or our condition straight with just a word. I thank God that He still moves suddenly.

Pentecost is about His <u>presence</u> and our praise. The text says a violent wind came from Heaven and filled the whole house where they were sitting and all of them were filled with the Holy Spirit and began to speak in other tongues.

When we've been in the presence of God, there should be some evidence when we've been in the presence of God.
- We should talk differently.
- We should act differently.
- We should feel differently.
- We should look differently.
- We should praise differently.
- We should walk differently.

When you've been in the presence of God, something should happen. When they were filled with God's presence, they responded by opening up their mouths in praise. How do you respond when you're in God's presence?

Rev. Dr. James E. Jones, Jr.

Live Free from Fear: A Prayer

Today, I begin my new walk free from fear because
I have been through enough and God is near.
I am no longer afraid to face each day because
I have lived long enough to know God will make a way.
Starting today I am free from any fears
It feels so good because I've doubted myself for so many years
With everything inside of me,
I know that God will take care of me.
From this day forward, I will not pout or doubt because
I know the Lord is going to bring me out
So I celebrate being me
And the fact that God has set me free.
Amen